Dirk Denison **10 Houses**

Dirk Denison
10 Houses

Fred A. Bernstein
Dirk Denison

Actar
New York / Barcelona

Contents

Preface

Fred A. Bernstein

The first time I met Dirk was over dinner in Chicago, and I remember the location clearly: L2O, the restaurant he created as a setting for the celebrated chef Laurent Gras. Dirk had designed every inch of the restaurant, including the carpets, the tables, and the chairs, and it all fit together like an elaborate 3-D puzzle. His attention to detail was astonishing, and the meal, already superb, was enhanced by the close fit between the food and its surroundings.

As I came to know Dirk's work during the next few years, I saw that same attention to detail over and over. Commissioned by a magazine to write about his Marin house, I encountered a building that was informed by architectural history but avoided architectural hubris. The design certainly owed a debt to Mies van der Rohe. But the real inspiration was Max, the clients' son, who was born with cerebral palsy and needed a house that was entirely barrier-free. Mies's idea of universal space and Max's need for universal access came together in an extraordinarily elegant building.

Later, writing for another magazine, I told the story of the house in Carmel that Dirk created for Kathy and Gary Bang, who had decided to downsize – really downsize, from 15,000 square feet on 150 acres to 1,800 square feet on 1/10th of an acre. Kathy described, among Dirk's many inventions, a meditation room that doubles as a guest room. She told me that under the tatami mats there is a TempurPedic mattress and that linens are stowed in a little drawer beneath the window seat. Tellingly, she said "The house is perfect for us. It's not a lot of space, but it's the right space." Dirk had created a house that was as tailored to the Bangs' needs as an item of clothing.

Over the next few years, I visited many more of Dirk's houses, and as I did, it never occurred to me that he should stick to any one style. After all, he had more than one client, and each client brought a unique set of needs and desires. That doesn't mean Dirk shortchanged his art, but rather that he worked to connect his clients' needs to larger architectural ideas, producing a range of successful solutions.

When we decided to work together on a book, I began by asking Dirk how his interest in architecture had developed. Soon I was captivated by his tales of meeting some of the most important American architects of the second half of the 20th century, from Gordon Bunshaft to Minoru Yamasaki to Peter Eisenman – even Louis Kahn, who came to his house for dinner. I realized that our conversation could become the backbone of a book. Over the next two years, we met in Chicago, where he lives, in New York, where I live, and in California, where he has done some of his most important work. Our conversation ranged from his early influences to his education and his many years in practice.

Dirk and I are almost the same age. We both attended the 1964–65 New York *World's Fair* with our parents, and we might literally have crossed paths walking from the Unisphere to Walt Disney's "it's a small world" to the Kodak pavilion's surreal landscape. If not, we crossed paths in other ways. Dirk became an architect and (after a few detours) I became an architecture writer, both of us having been deeply impressed during our childhood visits to the *World's Fair* by how surprising, inventive, and just plain fun architecture could be.

Between House and Home

Dirk Denison

'Home' is the space in which we live our lives, the places that are fundamental to who we are – our home town, our home room at school, our home page, our home screen, and even our home planet. These are places of beginnings, places that shape us, and places that we carry with us, in one way or another, wherever we go. Home describes our aspirations for arriving or returning – we are homeward bound, in the home stretch, sliding into home plate, or simply home free. Home is ultimately both the actual place and a metaphor for the sense of well-being, ease, intimacy, comfort, or familiarity that we know as feeling 'at home' with a particular person or in a particular place.

While 'home' simultaneously refers to the places in which we dwell and expresses a broader idea that is emblematic of our most elemental feelings and inner being, 'house' has a much narrower range of meaning, referring to the buildings in which we reside. As an architect who has a fundamental dedication to residential design, I find myself operating at the intersection of the two all the time. When a client commissions us to design their house, our goal is also to participate in the creation of their home by way of a complex and collaborative process that is part rigorous problem-solving exercise and part magic. Our clients themselves are central to the process, playing a variety of roles from informant to collaborator to sounding board. The key to the success of this collaboration between architect and client is the establishment of a relationship that allows us to work in close proximity, to generate ideas and share them, to work out problems and open doors instead of closing them.

In parallel with an extended conversation between myself and journalist Fred A. Bernstein, this volume presents ten houses, each one the final product of just such a highly interactive design and working process – a purposeful, rigorous, joyful, and sometimes messy affair that is ultimately concealed behind the 'clean' images wrought by the photographers with whom we work. When I look at the images of these houses, I see my clients, of course, but I also see the whole community of professionals who collaborated with us: the contractors, landscape architects, craftspeople from many different trades, artists and their galleries, furniture fabricators, design and engineering consultants, as well as members of zoning commissions and architectural review committees. Every one of these individuals and agencies has made essential contributions to the project.

When clients come to my office, that decision alone says something about them. It says that they aspire to a home that is unique and anticipates their future. What I love about designing houses is that it is a joint enterprise, it is optimistic, and it bears the promise of making lifelong dreams come true. Finding the core design idea for each residential project in a personal dream has been a focus of my work for three decades. Naturally, this goal extends to all the buildings I design, whether galleries, restaurants, dormitories, or offices, but looking back across almost a hundred completed projects, I realize that the private home is the building type that is most likely to fully express a client's dream. The first house presented here, for example, occupies a spectacular setting on the shores of Lake Michigan. It was conceived not only as a sanctuary for a couple and a hostel for their extended family of children and grandchildren, but also as a venue where music, debates, and education could take place in the company of family, friends, and community. In the course of designing and building the house, I learned from my clients about biomedical chemistry and family, and my clients learned from me about architecture and art. Together we shared food, dance, good company, and the richness of life.

Growing up, I lived in what I came to realize was the American suburb at its best, an encyclopedia of building styles from Tudor to gingerbread to ultra-modern. I was fortunate to also experience houses that were architecturally distinctive and filled with art. My interest in architecture developed early on. I played with Lincoln Logs and Legos and built forts out of bed sheets and refrigerator boxes, like most children, but what began to grow into a passionate interest in architecture was recognized and taken seriously by my parents right from the start. They invested themselves in making it possible for me to experience a wide range of places and buildings, and also introduced me to architects and designers, artists and dancers who were all wrestling with questions about space.

But it was my arts-oriented education at Cranbrook that galvanized my interests and experiences. Cranbrook was the result of the shared dream of a patron and an architect who worked together to create a community in which creativity would be cultivated and nourished. It remains an unparalleled example of an institution dedicated to the interconnectedness of design. Despite its suburban locale, Cranbrook belonged to metropolitan Detroit, which was our city when I was growing up. The Detroit of my childhood was literally alive with culture. Its vital commercial and manufacturing sectors nurtured architecture and industrial design along with the fine and performing arts. Looking back, I realize that the city literally shaped me, as a place. And to know Detroit in its glory and then witness its decline forced me to internalize the fact that places change over time, and also how profoundly the places we live affect us both individually and collectively.

I was educated as an architect at the Illinois Institute of Technology (IIT), where I now teach. Going from Detroit and Cranbrook to Chicago and IIT was a matter of moving from Saarinen to Mies, from Arts and Crafts, neo-Egyptian, and Art Deco to pure modernism. But the strongest parallel was the *placeness* with which both IIT and Cranbrook were imbued, both clearly the result of established objectives. In each case, the physical environment of the campus – buildings as well as landscapes – strongly influenced the educational experience. My rigorous architectural training at IIT was amplified by the very different educational approach of the Graduate School of Design at Harvard and then by my work in a number of architecture offices before I began teaching and later founded my own office.

For architects, like most creative professionals, education plays an ongoing role in practice. Education is a constant give-and-take that is mirrored in the give-and-take of professional life. My experience as a student of the visual and performing arts shaped and reshaped my understanding of the urban, suburban, and ex-urban realms. In parallel, these experiences formed the basis of my sensitivity to community and my commitment to education as the foundation of life, which extend through my work and the direction of my office to my relationships with clients, my teaching, my engagement with cultural institutions in Detroit, Chicago, and New York, and last but not least, my private life. For it is in my own life that all of this comes together in relationships based on sharing, learning, and working together.

Good design demands a conversation. At the heart of this book is the conversation Fred initiated, which unfolded as a natural extension of the way I work. Each commission brings its own set of needs and desires, the root of which can only be gotten to through the kind of discovery that comes from committed, collaborative dialogue. This leads to knowing how to ask the right questions, how to intuit the architectural problem fully, how to devise a compelling solution, how to lead clients through the complexity of building a house, and how to respond to whatever issues arise along the way. Each of my clients is unique, and as a result, the ten houses profiled in this book do not adhere to any one style. Designing every house using the same architectural vocabulary, effectively building a 'brand', has not been the goal of my practice; rather, we focus on 'getting it right', which in my mind means delivering the physical manifestation of the client's desires and needs, creating a place that expresses their idea of home and makes their life more pleasant and more meaningful, taking into account how they live now and how they might live in the future. The ultimate proof lies in the act of coming home and feeling content and fulfilled by the spirit of a house.

Acknowledgments

Architecture is a collaborative undertaking, from beginning to end. The team of extremely talented architects who make up our office put in very long hours, put up with a demanding boss, and work tirelessly to achieve excellence. Each member of the team makes invaluable contributions – from developing architectural ideas to tightening the details, tracking the progress of construction, installing furniture and art, and even settling our clients into their new homes. In particular, it has been my very good fortune to collaborate with the outstanding architects who took the lead on the ten houses presented in this volume – Michael Flath, Jacob Dodds, Todd Webb, Jason Dobbin, Rick (Richard) Nelson, and Michael Pierry.

I would also like to acknowledge and extend thanks to our collaborators beyond the office, who work no less tirelessly and with whom we share in the struggles as well as the accomplishments:

The allied creative professions with whom we work in ways that allow us to learn from one another as we evolve ideas and develop solutions, including Structural and Site Engineering Design – Jim (James M.) Kirk of Enspect and Paul Endres of Endrestudio, who taught us how to hang a house out over a bluff; Building Engineering Systems and Environmental Design – Jim (James R.) Bess in Chicago, with whom I've worked on every project since I founded my office; Lighting Design – Mitchell B. Kohn; Adrian Luchini, my collaborator on Pine Lake; Interior Design – Leslie Brush in northern California and Kerry Wilson in New York, both clients with whom I collaborated on the interiors, and Leslie Jones, with whom we have shared an office for over twenty years; Landscape Architecture – Julie Siegel in Evanston, Maria Smithburg, Doug Hoerr, and Mimi McKay in Chicago, and Andrea Cochran in San Francisco; Landscape Contractors – Mariani Landscape and Scott Byron and Co., both in Lake Bluff; General Contractors – Jeff Jozwiak at Norcon Inc., Jake (Jacob) Goldberg of Goldberg General Contracting, Inc., and Howard Dardick at Tip Top Builders in Chicago, Todd Altounian of Altounian Builders in Lake Bluff, Dan (Daniel) DeVito at DPD Builders, Ltd. in New York, Jay Blumenfeld of Redhorse Constructors, Inc. in San Francisco, Thomas H. George Construction in Carmel, and Frank Piku, our client who was also the general contractor.

The photographers who capture the character and context, but also the more elusive qualities of our work: Balthazar Korab (1926–2013), whom I met as a child, and who later documented my architectural models at IIT and eventually photographed the Pine Lake house, and those we work with currently, including Tom Harris, Eric Laignel, George Lambros, Michelle Litvin, David Matheson, Josh McHugh, Tom Rossiter, and Bill Zbaren.

I would also like to acknowledge and thank everyone who participated in the making of this book:

Fred Bernstein, from whom I learned so much in the course of a seemingly endless conversation carried on while we traveled together to visit each of the houses. Ramon Prat and Ricardo Devesa of Actar, our publishers, for generously supporting this project from its inception; members of our office staff who conducted crucial research, cataloging, and archiving of source materials; book designer Lorraine Wild, with whom I share history in Detroit and at Cranbrook, and her collaborator Ching Wang of Green Dragon; editorial consultant Denise Bratton; and Tyler Waldorf, managing director of my office, without whom this book would not have been possible.

Those who generously gave of their time to read and comment on the manuscript at different points along the way, including Ted Fishman, Victoria Lautman, Casey Jones, Walter Denison, Ellen Levy, and David Williams.

For their support and encouragement all along the way, I would like to extend very special thanks to:

Michele Oka Doner, Fred Eychaner, Helyn Goldenberg, Robin Goldsmith, Reed Kroloff, Jason Pickleman, Zoë Ryan, my colleagues in the College of Architecture and our team at the Mies Crown Hall Americas Prize at IIT, and my family, especially my father and Kathleen Denison, my sisters Tina and Nancy, and my niece Elizabeth.

And finally, my partner in all things, David Salkin.

George Gough Booth (1864–1949), who founded Cranbrook, believed that “the only thing worth finding is opportunity.” The story that unfolds in this book revolves around the many individuals who have granted me varied and unique opportunities – my parents and family, my teachers and mentors, in particular Myron Goldsmith, George Schipporeit, and Gene Summers, my much-valued collaborators, and all of my clients, especially whose who graciously allowed us to publish their homes here.

Dirk Denison

Dirk Denison and Fred A. Bernstein, a Conversation

I'd like to explore your early influences. What was the first house you remember?

I grew up in a simple, Foursquare house – basically a cube with four rooms to a floor – in a middle-class section of Birmingham, Michigan, a suburb of Detroit. [Fig. 1] There were sidewalks and backyard swings. But it wasn't Levittown – no two houses were alike. Our neighbors the Saffels, for example, lived in a clapboard house painted blue. The Watts house had an arched front door. My parents, Mary and Walter Denison, had chosen a red brick one with a wide front porch. Living there made me aware of the fact that a house could express a person's or a family's individuality and become part of how one saw oneself and presented oneself to the world.

Who was the first architect you met?

When I was around eight, my mother decided to renovate our kitchen. She hired Leo Hagan, an architect and furniture designer who had moved to Michigan to work with Eero Saarinen and later became the resident interior architect for IBM. The kitchen he designed was beautifully simple. It was centered on a 12-foot-long island with workspaces on one side and seating on the other. My mother was petite, about 5 feet 2 inches, so he dropped the counter to about 32 inches (from the normal height of 36), which meant he had to set the dishwasher in a hole in the floor. He brought the upper cabinets down as well so that she could reach them easily. The countertops were made of white Formica, a material I'd never seen before. I remember other details, too. For example, to create space for spice jars and canned goods, Hagan opened one wall down to the studs and installed between them 4-inch shelves enclosed with beautiful teak doors. Every inch of available space was put to use. My sense of the potential for customization, of a unique relationship between the user and the design of a house, derives from that experience. It awakened in me a sense of how creatively an architect could work with a client.

1

You watched everything that was going on?

Yes, and the construction process fascinated me. Hagan tore out much of the back of the house, and I would climb through the opening every day when I came home from school to see what had been done. The demolition made me aware of the many layers that make up a wall, but also showed me that even what seemed like a fixed part of a building wasn't inviolable.

So walls came down?

Yes, the new kitchen combined what had been three smaller rooms, and it was fascinating to see one space become part of another. As for the back of the house, Hagan installed a series of picture windows, which he composed almost like a Mondrian painting. This gave the interior a whole new relationship to the backyard.

Was that the only kind of house you knew?

No, because not far from us in Bloomfield Hills was a Frank Lloyd Wright house commissioned by Melvyn Maxwell Smith and Sarah Stein Smith, who were friends of my grandparents. It was a tiny Usonian house on a pretty pond (1950). [Fig. 2] When I visited them, they talked about how they had selected Wright, what it was like to work with him, and the pleasure they took in the domestic conditions he created for them. I was

2

fascinated by the library at the center of the house and how much functionality Wright could insert into that tiny space. It had a desk, a bench, and bookshelves, but the whole room was only 5 by 6 feet. A series of built-ins gave the living room a welcoming appearance. In particular, there was a banquette running the length of the inside wall. It provided comfortable seating, but also directed the eye out into the landscape. [Fig. 3] That was also my first exposure to glass that went from the floor to the ceiling, so that the interior space appeared to extend beyond the building. One other thing that has stayed with me: on the street side, the house was set into a mound of earth, which made it seem like part of the topography. Visitors had to search for the entrance, and after being admitted to the house, had to duck beneath a low ceiling – it couldn't have been more than 7 feet high. After that, the living room ceiling, which was probably only 9 feet high, seemed to soar. It was my first exposure not only to the spatial technique of compression and release, but also the idea that architecture is a series of spatial experiences.

3

What did you learn from visiting the Smiths?

Most people I know moved into a finished house, then shopped for furniture. I was struck by how different Wright's approach was, with all of the furnishing components integrated into the architectural design. And I loved how the architecture embraced the landscape. But most of all, I appreciated how the architecture was inseparable from the Smiths themselves. The house became a defining element of their lives.

4

What other kinds of houses did you see as a child?

In the 1950s and 1960s, as I was growing up, Detroit was exploding with creativity. Architects were expressing this optimism by embracing modernism. William Kessler and Philip Meathe of Meathe, Kessler & Associates were important in this great modernist trajectory. They did a series of elegant glass boxes on wonderful sites, such as Kessler's Hilbert H. DeLawter house in Bloomfield Hills (1962). [Fig. 4] Their work, with sheets of glass stretching from floor to ceiling enclosing simple volumes, helped prepare me for my later encounters with the work of Mies van der Rohe.

Do you remember a particular Meathe, Kessler house?

My mother took me to see the house W. Hawkins Ferry commissioned in Grosse Point Shores. It had been published on the cover of the September 1969 issue of *House Beautiful*. Ferry was the heir to a great seed company fortune. His parents were founders of the Detroit Institute of Arts (DIA), to which Ferry himself had donated some very important pieces. My mother, through her work for the DIA, must have gone to a meeting at the house and asked if she could come back with her son, "who's interested in architecture." So we went over. Back then, Grosse Pointe was very staid, very traditional, with huge chateaus and palazzos, and then there was Ferry's white steel box designed by William Kessler (1964). [Fig. 5] My reaction, as we drove up, was "What is this? This

5

does not look like a house." There were two-story windows facing Lake St. Clair. I had never seen glass on that scale. Inside, there was a conversation pit, like at Eero Saarinen's J. Irwin Miller house in Columbus, Indiana (1957). There were works by Arp, Calder, Giacometti, Gottlieb, and Picasso – all great artists – and a sculptural stairway that was an artwork in itself, a helical stack of curved marble slabs rising toward a futuristic skylight.

6

Did you spend time with the owner?

Yes, and Ferry was the most extraordinary person I had ever met – especially striking to a teenager just beginning to realize he was gay. When he spoke, every word was pronounced and exaggerated, but he was not pretentious. He was a generous spirit, who seemed happy to meet a young person who liked art and architecture. He was a Harvard-trained architect and architectural historian who wrote the definitive book on Detroit architecture, *The Buildings of Detroit: A History* (1968), as well as *The Legacy of Albert Kahn* (1970), the first monograph on the father of industrial architecture. I remember so clearly the way the house underscored who Ferry was. When we visited him, we came up a long drive to the entrance. A housekeeper opened a pair of tall doors. Inside, we crossed beneath a balcony and passed the stairway to reach the edge of the sunken conversation pit. Suddenly we were greeted by a comforting voice from above as he leaned over the edge of the balcony to offer words of welcome. [Fig. 6] His environment was simply an extension of his being.

How long did your family stay in the red brick house?

When I was about ten, my mother decided we should move. It was time to have more than one bathroom for the family. There was also a desire for more outdoor space, and for a house that had more character, more presence – the same reasons clients come to me today. From then on, almost every weekend, my mother would take me with her to look at houses. It became a sort of hobby. Even then I loved sketching, and I was always suggesting modifications to the houses we saw. Sometimes, I would take the realtors' plans and draw right on them. I think our house-hunting experience was what really cemented my interest in residential architecture.

Was there a particular style you liked?

I had a secret love for Tudor. Partly that had to do with the amount of detail – the stone carving, the wood balusters, the nooks and crannies. Each room had its own character. There was a sense of discovery as you moved around.

It sounds like you saw a lot of great houses.

Yes, and long before I studied architecture, I was aware of the different feelings that each of the houses gave me.

What kind of house did your parents ultimately buy?

It was a southern Georgian Colonial, a big house from the 1920s with red tile floors, stucco walls detailed with pecan wood, and heavy carved handrails on the stairway. It was the site that decided it. The house had a beautiful rear yard that sloped down to the only lake in Birmingham, a mill pond within walking distance of downtown, which was important to my mother. I think that at heart, my mother preferred modern houses. The advantage of a traditional house was that there were endless walls for art.

7

What was your own room like?

I had seven aquariums in my bedroom as a kid. There were all different kinds of fish, saltwater and freshwater. Being able to press up against the glass and watch all of that was a way of connecting with nature, and also a way for a shy boy to enter into a world that was available and beautiful, but not threatening. By the time I was a teenager, we went to Bloomingdale's and bought a suite of the cardboard furniture Frank Gehry designed (ca. 1972), which I still have. [Fig. 7]

And how was the rest of the house furnished?

Much of the space was devoted to art, including works derived from everyday objects. Guests would ask my mother "What? You have a giant tea bag?" – referring to a Claes Oldenburg. She also had a watercolor of a Coca-Cola bottle and a Campbell's Soup can by Andy Warhol, both of which she acquired on a visit to The Factory in the early 1960s. There were artifacts from my father's travels, too – African tribal masks and tables inlaid with ivory from India.

Your mother liked pop art?

I think she liked pop artists. Every piece in her collection was made by someone she had met and was able to have a conversation with and get to know before acquiring the work. She was always having artists over to the house. It was nonstop. When I was in high school, Detroit was an art Mecca. In and around the Cass Corridor, which is part of inner-city Detroit, works like Ellen Phelan's *Untitled* (*Blouse*) (ca. 1971) and Gordon Newton's *Untitled* (1971), as well as works by Aris Koutroulis (*1985 – #24*) and McArthur Binion (*dna: white painting: test for seasons XII*, 2016) exemplified a wave of creativity that was partly fueled by Sam Wagstaff, then curator of modern and contemporary art at the DIA. [Figs. 8, 9, 10, and 11] Sam and my mother were close, and the whole idea of the potential for art to provoke new thinking was very much under discussion in our living room. Sam's explorations culminated in Michael Heizer moving a block of granite across the

8

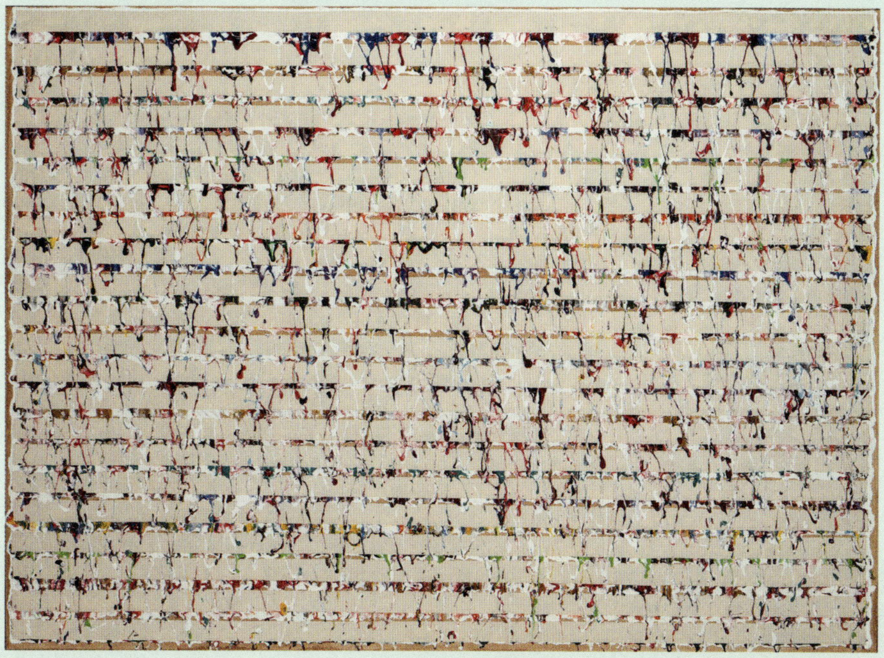

10

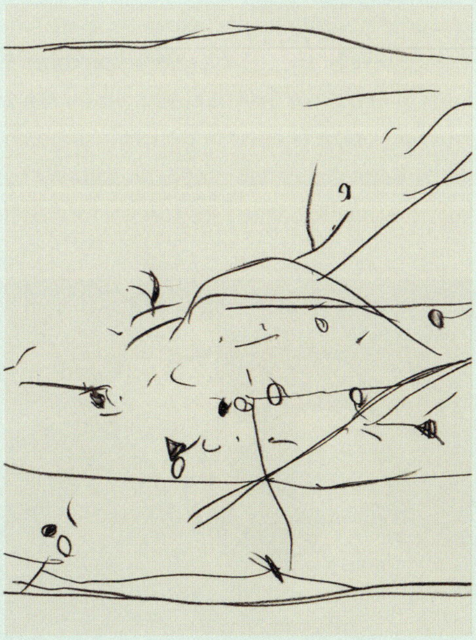

9

11

12

front lawn of the DIA – his *Dragged Mass Geometric* of 1971 – while I stood and watched. [Fig. 12] There was a great outcry from the general public, who saw the piece as a sort of destructive act. This of course led to Wagstaff leaving Detroit for New York.

My mother was interested in the whole spectrum of performing arts. In Detroit, she co-founded a contemporary dance initiative, the Metropolitan Dance Project, which brought great choreographers like Merce Cunningham with John Cage, José Limón, Alvin Ailey, and others to the city. They also came to Cranbrook and led master classes in choreography, not just dance, for a troupe I belonged to at the time. I later brought some of these methods into my own teaching at IIT. My 'placemaking' classes included having students move around Crown Hall in ways that helped them understand the relationship between their bodies and architectural space. These classes culminated in a performance staged in a landscape my students and I created. Choreographers Alejandro Cerrudo, Lucas Crandall, and Brian Enos worked under Hubbard Street Dance artistic director Jim Vincent to create original works. [Fig. 13]

Your mother sounds like Auntie Mame.

13

She devoted her life to creative pursuits. She was a long-time governor of the Cranbrook Academy of Art and a trustee of the DIA, not because she donated a million dollars – we didn't have a million dollars – but because she was so passionate about art. She also ran a nonprofit artist space called the Detroit Artists Market in the inner city and motivated the Junior League to focus on contemporary art, which was a coup. She was a great character. When I was young, she bought her clothes at Yves Saint-Laurent's Rive Gauche shop on East 71st Street in Manhattan. She wore Saint-Laurent when she and my father attended the opening of *Hair* at the Vest Pocket Theater in Detroit in June 1970. [Fig. 14] Eventually, she began wearing pieces by Bette Appel, who made everything out of sweatshirt material. My mother went from very structured to very free-form, a total Bohemian.

14

Lake Michigan

Lake Michigan

You mentioned artists and choreographers.
Did she invite architects to the house as well?

While I was in high school, Louis Kahn lectured at the DIA. My mother invited him to the house for dinner.

What was dinner with Louis Kahn like?

Well, he asked me if I drew, and I said yes, and he asked me if I liked science, and I said science was my favorite subject. I remember him talking about the world as a kind of ticking bomb, and how we were naive not to realize the potential for conflict as different cultures interacted. That made sense to me at the time. In school, we were learning about ecology, joining the Sierra Club, and raising money for UNICEF to combat world-wide hunger – our concern for the world was genuine and quite pronounced. It was the 1960s! There was a planetary consciousness of all humanity being interconnected. Even so, I think I was a bit surprised by the person of Kahn himself, who was somewhat awkward, a little bit shy, and definitely quirky. Not the image a teenager might have of a great master.

15

16

I loved Kahn's work. We went to Fort Worth to see the Kimbell Museum in 1972, right after it was completed. [Fig. 15] It was the most beautiful museum I had ever seen. I experienced the Kimbell as an institutional building at a residential scale, an inherently human scale. The thing that was most moving for me was the wash of natural light over the concrete barrel arch, and the use of materials – the concrete structure juxtaposed with oak paneling on the inside and travertine on the outside. I also loved the courtyard with the fountain. [Fig. 16] Later, my best friend from middle school, John Murphy, was studying at Yale and rented a loft across from Kahn's Center for British Art (completed 1977), which we watched being built from his window. [Fig. 17]

17

Apart from Leo Hagan and Louis Kahn, did you know any other architects?

My mother's best friend from high school was Robin Goldsmith. I call her 'Aunt Robin'. Her husband was Myron Goldsmith, a partner at Skidmore, Owings & Merrill (SOM) in Chicago. Before he went to SOM, he worked for Mies. He was essentially responsible for ensuring that Mies's Farnsworth house in Plano, Illinois, (1945–51) got built by maintaining the relationship between Mies and the client, Edith Farnsworth – quite an achievement. [Fig. 18]

18

And you spent a lot of time with Myron Goldsmith?

My parents would put my sister Tina and myself on a plane and send us off to see the Goldsmiths, who lived in a Victorian house in Wilmette, just north of Chicago. Myron would take me to see whatever buildings he was excited about at the time. One I remember was an Illinois Bell Telephone (IBT) switching station, out in Northbrook, Illinois (1974). [Fig. 19] It was a little windowless box with a gridded black facade. What distinguished it was how rigorously it was done. The architect was Gerald Horn, who had come out of Craig Ellwood's office in California and became head of design at Holabird & Root in Chicago. I ended up not only studying with Gerald Horn at IIT, but also working with him at Holabird & Root one summer. Myron took me seriously, even when I was a kid. He drove me around Chicago to show me SOM's new work. I remember seeing the Sears Tower (now Willis Tower, 1973) under construction. [Fig. 20] He also took me to see most of Mies's buildings in Chicago. On one trip, I watched Alexander Calder's *Flamingo* being installed on Mies's Federal Plaza (1974). [Fig. 21]

19

20

21

22

On another, we went to IIT, to see Crown Hall (1950–56). [Fig. 22] The idea of a building that just sort of floats made a strong impression on me. Myron had designed the Republic Newspaper Building (1971) in Columbus, Indiana, and we visited that as well as the town, which sits in the middle of farm country but is filled with buildings by great modern architects. [Fig. 23] In my early impressions of the project of modernism, Columbus was the counterweight to the architecture I had seen as a child at the New York *World's Fair* in 1964 and *Expo 67* in Montréal – it was real and permanent. Columbus also showed me what a single great client, Irwin Miller, could accomplish. Meanwhile, my parents had given me the Mies van der Rohe drawings portfolio published by the Museum of Modern Art (1964) for my twelfth birthday. I thought it was amazing. I would spend all day looking at the plans, thinking, "These are drawings of buildings, but they're also art." The portfolio contained not only line drawing, plans, and elevations, but also collage, a medium traditionally used by artists, which Mies used for example to represent his project for the Georg Schaefer Museum in Schweinfurt (1960–63). [Fig. 24] So Myron, who was very close to Mies, arranged for me to meet him. I was to bring the portfolio, and he would sign it.

23

24

What happened?

Mies died that year, in August 1969, just before we were supposed to meet.

What else did you learn from Myron?

For Myron, architecture was a serious art. He was a progenitor of the idea that there was beauty in expressing pure structure. His McMath-Pierce Solar Telescope at the Kitt Peak National Observatory in Arizona (1962), for example, is the perfect amalgamation of form and function. [Fig. 25] These ideas had their foundation in the thesis he wrote under Mies on the effects of scale on structure – a thesis that in my opinion influenced Mies's late work. He always described buildings with reference to what the architect's goals were, and whether the finished product supported those goals. He would talk about whether the building was or wasn't "working."

25

So you owe him a lot?

It was Myron's passion that made me so certain that I wanted to become an architect.

26

Did you meet any other architects in Bloomfield Hills?

I knew the client for Peter Eisenman's 1975 House X – Janet Aronoff, the aunt of my very close friend Ellen Levy, whom I later took to the senior prom at Cranbrook. Janet knew I was interested in architecture, and invited me over to see Eisenman's proposal. [Fig. 26] What I saw were the most spectacular architectural drawings and models imaginable – a totally new and unfamiliar architecture. But the next time I inquired about the house, she said, "We're not doing it." She ended up buying a French chateau. I never quite found out what happened. Later, when I was studying with Peter at Harvard, he told me that when she decided not to move forward, he was "crushed."

You've talked a lot about your mother. What was the rest of your family like?

Everyone was socially and environmentally conscious. My mother's father was a family court judge, and he and my grandmother would always invite kids who were in foster care to dinner. They also started a residence for disadvantaged children. They were Republicans who thought that individuals – not government – should take care of the indigent. And they did just that, looking out for people who were going through hard times. It's not surprising that my sister Tina is a social worker.

And your father?

My father has devoted himself to education, historic preservation, and community service organizations. He is a very hard worker who believes it is important to have structure in your life. So, for instance, he believed that if we didn't make our beds in the morning, our days would be unproductive. That ethos is reflected in my work, which amounts to a series of efforts to help people find structure.

What did he do professionally?

27

He was a lawyer who worked long hours, but he also loved the outdoors. His father had property in the woods in Grayling, in upper Michigan, where we went year-round. [Fig. 27] We stayed in a bunkhouse; the outhouse was across the road. There were lots of projects to do outdoors – clearing brush, building a bridge over a stream. For me, these experiences established a lifelong relationship with nature. But more than that, my father was and still is a great adventurer. In 1948, he and his father went to Africa on the first safari after the Second World War. It was planned for them by Thomas Cook. A few years later, he and a group of international hunters founded one of the largest wild-life conservation organizations in the world, the Shikar-Safari Club International Foundation, to protect indigenous species and their environments. He is still active in the organization, actually.

Your parents sound like real live wires.

It's true. Both of my parents were adventurous, my mother embracing art, design, and the performing arts, and my father the spectacles of nature. The many trips we took to look at architecture as well as the national parks across the United States encouraged my sense of wonderment. Both my mother and my father were voracious readers, but they somehow knew that a love of architecture and nature was nourished less by reading than actual experience, so they immersed me in the 'real thing'.

What were some of the adventures you remember?

My parents took me to the 1964-65 *World's Fair* in New York. I was only seven, but I remember being fascinated by the site plan, with Gilmore David Clark's Unisphere at the center and all the pavilions arrayed around it on radial paths. [Fig. 28] It gave me a taste of what *A Century of Progress* in Chicago (1933–34) might have been like, or even more seminal fairs like the *Exposition universelle* in Paris (1889), with the Eiffel Tower, or the *Great Exhibition* in London (1851), with the Crystal Palace. There was an optimism that appealed to me. It was still a time of surprises; each thing you came upon was new and exciting.

28

At the New York *World's Fair*, technology was the star – the 'moving sidewalk' taking you past Michelangelo's *Pietà* (on loan from the Vatican); General Electric's Progressland pavilion with the 'revolving auditorium' called the Carousel of Progress; the ingenuity of Walt Disney's "it's a small world after all." But it was also a celebration of architecture. The pavilions were incredibly diverse, constructed using all kinds of materials and deploying unusual shapes – spherical, like the Unisphere, cylindrical like the Astral Fountain, also by Gilmore David Clark, and free-form, like Victor Lundy's *Space Flowers* mounted on the roof of one of the Brass Rail snack bars. [Figs. 29 and 30] Imagine how new that all looked to me, having grown up in the Foursquare house! It was amazing to discover how free and inventive architecture could be.

29

30

31

Three years later, we went to Montréal for *Expo 67*. It wasn't as exuberant as the New York fair, but it was even more potent for me because of some of the individual works of architecture. Of course we saw Buckminster Fuller's Biosphère. [Fig. 31] I remember being amazed that such a light skin could enclose such a huge volume. There was the fun of riding the gondola that went through, up, and around the dome, but also the more consequential realization that buildings could contain ecosystems. It was something like the Ford Foundation Building in New York, but on a larger scale. The most seminal experience was seeing Moshe Safdie's Habitat and realizing that those pieces could be made off-site, hoisted by cranes, and stacked up in a way that created a wide variety of exterior spaces. [Fig. 32] I remember thinking this is what I want to do with my life! The units you were allowed to enter had gorgeous textiles and warm oak finishes. They had a very comfortable feeling on the inside, in contrast to the roughness outside. Like so many moments in the history of prefabrication, Habitat didn't change the game. Prefabrication has not in the meantime become a prevalent mode of making architecture, but for me, it remains an important example of how standard units can be combined to create a more complex form.

32

Carmel

Where else did your parents take you?

My first trip to Europe was the same summer as *Expo 67*.

All this at age ten?

It was a busy summer! We started out in a small town near Geneva, where friends of ours were living. The town was tiny and tight, and looked like something from a storybook. The streets met at odd angles, so the houses had a lot of diagonals. So different from the Detroit suburbs I knew. From there we went to Italy. In Florence, we stayed in an old convent high above the city. The rooms were tiny, but we spent our time there on a porch that ran the length of the building. We'd have long quiet lunches, with no one hurrying us away to make room at the table. It was my first real exposure to leisure, very different from the constant push to be productive I was used to.

33

Probably most memorable, to a ten-year-old me, was the Ponte Vecchio. I was transfixed by the idea of shops suspended over the Arno River, and Giorgio Vasari's secret passageway overhead (1565) for Cosimo de' Medici to move back and forth between his residence in the Palazzo Pitti and the Palazzo Vecchio where he held court every day. [Fig. 33] There were further surprises in Rome, where the Pantheon and the ruins of the ancient Forum made the biggest impression on me, along with the engineering of the fountains in the terraced garden of the Villa d'Este in Tivoli. [Fig. 34] And Venice! To a child,

34

35

Venice was magical: a city on water! How does that work? The following year, my parents took me to visit the Grand Canyon and a number of other national parks. [Fig. 35] The year after that, in the spring of 1969, my class went on a study trip to Greece, because fifth-graders at Brookside elementary school at Cranbrook learned Greek and studied Greek history, art, and mythology.

I had a wide range of experiences with both natural and cultural wonders, but the biggest adventure came when I was 15, in 1972. My father took my mother, Tina, and myself to Africa. We spent three months traveling, much of it off-road. He wanted us to experience – to the extent possible – what he had experienced in 1948. Although the focus was wildlife, I have vivid memories of the buildings we saw, including a lodge in the Serengeti National Park in Tanzania, a modernist floating concrete roof supported on outcroppings of stone. So simple.

Was there hunting?

Yes, and it was difficult for me, but for my father, it was a rite of passage. The hunting was part of a well-managed program based on extreme consciousness of the status and fate of various species and their natural habitats. At the time there were 25,000 elephants on the Galana Ranch in Kenya, for example, and authorities were culling eighty or a hundred of them each year. If the park didn't meet that quota, the rangers would come in and cull the number they thought necessary to maintain the habitat. This was long before the advent of the poaching that ultimately decimated the elephant population in Africa.

Do you remember the cities?

Yes, particularly Dakar, in Senegal, our first stop, which to me felt like another world. The buildings were all concrete, with *brise soleil* and other features that acknowledged their tropical setting. I remember staying at the modernist Hôtel de N'Gor, a big slab, but it had skip-stop circulation, so you came off on one floor and there were stairs that went up and stairs going down, very much a reference to Le Corbusier, complete with high ceilings fitted with fans, because of course there was no air-conditioning. [Fig. 36] In South Africa, we saw apartheid in full force. I remember being shocked; it felt like people were

36

37

living in prisons. Then we traveled to what are now Zambia and Zimbabwe to see Victoria Falls. [Fig. 37] The last stop was Uganda. It was 1972, and Idi Amin was expelling or murdering non-Africans.

It's hard to picture your mother allowing you to go somewhere that dangerous.

My mother was in a certain sense the most adventurous of us all. All of my father's friends in Kenya were saying, "Don't go to Uganda." But Kampala was the last stop on the trip, and my mother said, "We came all this way, and we're going to go" – which almost got us killed.

What happened?

It was too dangerous for us to be in Kampala, so our driver hid us in the countryside. One day, there was a huge thunderstorm. He let us know that this was our opportunity. We all got into the car and he drove us straight to the airport. We went through two roadblocks where they waved us through only because they couldn't be bothered to stand out in the rain. When we got to the airport, there were only three boarding passes left, and the tarmac was crowded with people trying to get on the plane. It was chaos. Everyone was just piled with things like chickens and furniture. My mother, my sister, and I were able to get boarding passes, but only in the last moment before the plane took off did my father appear in the cabin. He had somehow negotiated a ticket, but he later told me we were lucky to get out with our lives.

Where did you go from there?

From Entebbe, we flew to Munich, arriving during the 1972 Summer Olympics, the day after the massacre of the Israeli athletes. We got off the plane and the airport was deserted except for soldiers with machine guns. We didn't know what had happened. It wasn't until we exited the airport and met our friends that they told us the whole story. I remember thinking, what kind of world are we living in? First Uganda and then Munich: how do you process all of that, coming from a suburb of Detroit?

Did you see any of the Olympics?

Yes, but I was as interested in the stadiums as the games themselves. Frei Otto and Günther Behnisch's Olympiastadion (1968–72), with its lighter-than-air canopies floating overhead, made me feel like I'd been transported to another world. [Fig. 38]

38

39

40

What was Detroit like?

Back then, it was a dynamic, forward-looking city. There was a great optimism that came full force into our everyday lives, driven by the technological innovation that was taking place all around us. At the same time, there were proud, established institutions. In those days, one wore a coat and tie to go shopping at Hudson's, which made the experience very special. We went to the theater in the great Art Deco Fisher Building by Joseph Nathaniel French of Albert Kahn Associates (1928). [Figs. 39 and 40] We also frequented the Detroit Institute of Arts, with its Diego Rivera murals and an entire colonial house installed inside the building. [Fig. 41] My mother often attended evening meetings at the DIA. Sometimes, she would take me along, and I would have free run of the whole place after hours.

41

And what do you remember of Detroit architecture?

Of course the Fisher Building loomed large, but there was also Albert Kahn's neoclassical General Motors Building (now Cadillac Place, 1923), which when it opened was one of the largest office buildings in the world. [Fig. 42] I also have great memories of going to father-son events at the Detroit Athletic Club (1915), a magnificent Renaissance revival building, also by Albert Kahn. [Fig. 43] At the same time, there were exciting modern buildings going up. The Michigan Consolidated Gas Company Building (now

42

43

One Woodward Avenue, 1963) by Minoru Yamasaki with Smith, Hinchman & Grylls (SHG) was his first really tall building. [Figs. 44 and 45] There was also the First Federal Savings and Loan Association Building by SHG (1965). [Fig. 46] Remember, in the late 1950s and early 1960s, Detroit was booming in the way that Silicon Valley is today.

44

45

46

Were you aware of what began to happen in the late 1960s?

Yes, the city started burning all around us on April 4, 1968, when Martin Luther King was assassinated in Memphis. My mother, being my mother, took us downtown to see what was going on. Only three weeks earlier, King had given one of his last speeches at Grosse Point High School.

How did the situation affect you?

It was like we lost our city. It was a terrible feeling, not only the fact that the site of my childhood memories was forever transformed, but also that society had failed. For my family, the focus had shifted to New York by that time.

Wilmette

FOOD
LA CUISINE VERTE

What did you see when you went to New York?

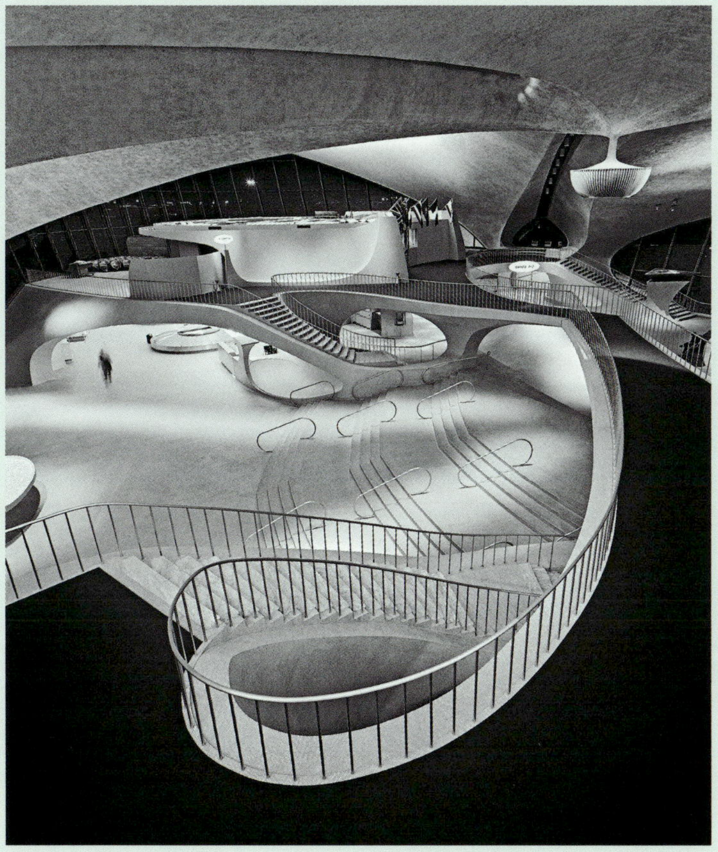

47

New York was about art and theater and new architecture. There were surprisingly powerful parallels between my experiences in the Midwest with Mies, Saarinen, SOM, and Yamasaki, among others, and what had been happening in New York – SOM's Lever House (1952), Mies's Seagram Building (1958), Saarinen's CBS Building (1965), and Yamasaki's World Trade Center (1973).

All office buildings!

Well, when we went to Europe in 1967, the portal was Eero Saarinen's TWA Flight Center (1962) at the JFK International Airport. [Fig. 47] But otherwise, you're right, this was a time when corporate architects were heroes. SOM was doing some of its best work and I. M. Pei was doing some of his best work. I remember being overwhelmed by Kevin Roche and John Dinkeloo's Ford Foundation Building (1968) on 42nd Street. [Fig. 48] This was a fertile period for modernism, before postmodernism entered the picture. Architects like Saarinen and Roche Dinkeloo were designing modernist corporate buildings inseparably tied to the character of their clients.

48

Did you meet any of the New York architects?

Myron introduced us to Gordon Bunshaft, who arranged visits to his Beinecke Rare Book and Manuscript Library at Yale (1960–63). [Fig. 49] We also visited the American Can Company Headquarters building in Greenwich, Connecticut (1970). And we already knew Yamasaki.

49

From Detroit?

Yes. I knew his architecture from a very early age. The McGregor Memorial Conference Center (1958) on the Wayne State University Campus was a gem. [Fig. 50] It added fanciful ornament to the Miesian vocabulary. I have already mentioned his Michigan Consolidated Gas Company building (1960–62), an office tower right on the waterfront. [Fig. 51] Both Yamasaki buildings were beautiful and optimistic, and I realized those are two things architecture could and should be. Building is a great act of confidence in the future – you can't do it unless you're optimistic.

50

51

How did you meet Yamasaki?

When I was about 13, my mother said, “Let’s go visit ‘Yama’ at his office.” So we did. I remember a big open space in a low building. In the middle of the space there must have been a hundred models of the World Trade Center. [Fig. 52] One tower, two towers, three towers, all different sizes and shapes. They had already decided on the twin tower scheme, which was something like scheme number 32, but they kept building more models. I asked Yamasaki why, and he said, “I wanted to make sure it was the right decision.” It was a very powerful lesson.

52

Let's talk about your formal education. You started out at Cranbrook?

Yes, I studied there from nursery school all the way through the twelfth grade. My delight in architecture was largely a product of the Cranbrook experience. I was not only conscious of the environment in which I was immersed, but I was encouraged to explore and appreciate it by my parents and my teachers.

What was it like?

Cranbrook was a whole ecosystem of lakes and valleys and woods and waterfalls. Brookside, the elementary school, had been designed by the school's founder, George Gough Booth, and his son Henry S. Booth. The earliest buildings on the campus included Bertram Goodhue's magnificent Christ Episcopal Church (1928, completed after his death) and the Booth family's country home, with its formal gardens, by Albert Kahn. But even more remarkable were the schools designed by Eliel Saarinen: not just his famous Academy of Art, the Art Museum and Library, and the Institute of Science, but also the Cranbrook School for Boys, which I attended, and the Kingswood School for Girls. [Fig. 53] Even as a kid I realized that Saarinen engaged in a form of total design, giving the same amount of thought to a doorknob as a site plan. That was an important lesson.

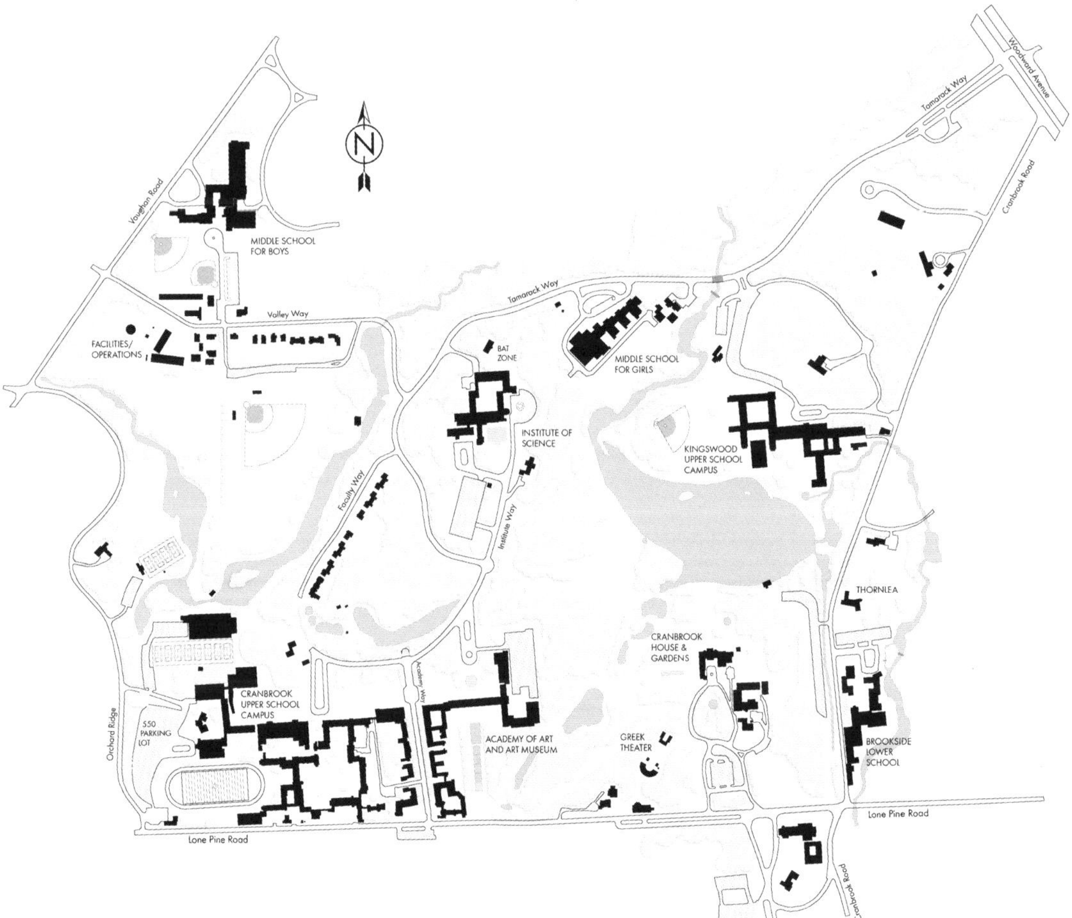

53

Tell me more about the grounds.

The Cranbrook campus is spread over more than 300 acres, all of it an extraordinary synthesis of landscape, architecture, sculpture, and water. Fountains and lakes were part of Saarinen's larger vision. [Figs. 54 and 55] He collaborated with his wife, Louise Gesellius, his son Eero, and the sculptor Carl Milles. Each part of the campus was designed in a very different vocabulary and put forward different ideas about the relationship between buildings and landscape.

54

55

56

57

The Cranbrook School for Boys (1928) was modeled on an English country village; Kingswood School for Girls (1931) was conceived as an Art Deco 'palace'; and the Academy of Art (1941) was designed in a neo-Egyptian style. [Figs. 57, 58, 59 and 56] There was a lot to discover, and there were endless ways to discover it. A fanciful trail would lead to stairs that went behind a hedgerow and suddenly brought you out at the top of a hill. Taking different routes would lead to very different experiences, all of which Saarinen had anticipated. It was a fertile setting for the active imagination.

59

58

60

Which building do you remember best?

The dining room at Cranbrook, where we ate lunch every day, was a masterpiece, a cathedral-like space with powerful concrete barrel vaults and spectacular lighting fixtures Saarinen designed and produced in collaboration with the Orrefors Glass Company in Sweden. The tall, barrel-vaulted windows, about fifty of them, were fitted with slender vertical panels of leaded glass. Every window was unique. [Fig. 60] On the exterior, Saarinen used a lot of 'clinker' bricks, which take on irregular shapes when they are fired. Some of the bricks were left protruding, some were laid sideways, so that there was a great diversity of texture to the wall surfaces. It was interesting to hear from the craftsmen who built the buildings, some of whom were still living and working there when I was growing up, that much of the artistic license for the masonry and woodworking and was left to them. The vision for Cranbrook was that of a utopian society insofar as everyone's contribution was valued.

Tell me about the Booth house.

The Booth family, founders of Cranbrook, commissioned Albert Kahn to design a house for them in the center of the family farm that became the campus. Kahn was known as the father of the assembly-line building, but he also did neo-traditional houses for leading families like the Dodges and the Fords. The Booth house, in an English Arts & Crafts style, was probably 25,000 square feet. I got to know the house well, because in the tenth grade, I helped develop a campus tour to celebrate Cranbrook's 50th anniversary, and spent a lot of time in that house interviewing Mr. Booth.

What was the education like?

In keeping with the physical surroundings that provided a surprise at every turn, Cranbook was an academic environment that nurtured creativity. It was a perfect stage for youth and adolescence, a place to dream up who you were or who you could or would be. There were teachers like Susan Rice, who taught us logic using Sherlock Holmes; there was John Gohegan, who showed us the potential of film to communicate powerful ideas; and the choreographer-dancer Jessica Sinclair, who taught us how our bodies exist in space. The latter became quite important to me as an architect. Not surprisingly, my classmates excelled at self-expression: Ellen Levy became a poet, John Murphy a painter, and Mary Lou Geiger a theatrical lighting designer – and there were many more. But for me, Cranbrook was academically challenging. Despite having great teachers, I was easily distracted as a child. I would sit in math class drawing plans.

Math class in particular?

In math class, we had graph paper. I was addicted to graph paper, which kept everything orthogonal.

Pine Lake

From Cranbrook, you went to the University of Michigan at Ann Arbor.

Yes. Every member of my family had gone to Michigan. It was a rite of passage.

What did you study?

I studied the history of art and architecture, and mathematics.

What do you remember of the campus?

61

Michigan was a sort of mish-mash of architecture from a lot of different eras, but when I arrived in 1975, there was already the Power Performing Arts Center (1971) by Kevin Roche and John Dinkeloo (where I played the role of the character who sings "Shipoopi" in *The Music Man*). [Fig. 61] Later, I had the opportunity to walk through the Allan and Alene Smith Law Library Addition (1981) with its architect, Gunnar Birkerts. [Fig. 62] The building was entirely underground, so as not to compete with the collegiate Gothic Law Quad. From that experience I learned a technique that I've used over and over in my own work: when a building or part of a building is underground, giving it two different sources of natural light reduces the sense of being below grade. Its distinguishing feature was its mirrored glass facade reflecting a grove of mature oak trees. The following year, Hugh Newell Jacobsen's Alumni Center (1982) was completed, the smartest feature of which was the way it replicated a diagonal footpath as an interior passageway.

62

And then?

After two years at Michigan, I took a year off to work at the large Detroit architecture firm Smith, Hinchman & Grylls (SHG, now the Smith Group). I worked in the hospital division, where I learned that certain parts of certain buildings, such as operating rooms, were successful when they were derived from projects with a proven record of performance, while other parts of a building wanted to be fresh and new and different.

Where did you go after Smith, Hinchman & Grylls?

Myron Goldsmith said, "It's time to take architecture seriously," which to him meant "come to IIT." After Mies died, Myron was the guiding spirit there.

And you did?

Yes. I did the five-year B. Arch program there. I could have skipped ahead a year or two, but I wanted to have the full experience. It was 1978, and the sequential and iterative curriculum Mies conceived was still in place.

Can you describe the curriculum?

63

In the architecture studio, we didn't start with buildings. First we drew a straight line freehand, then a straight line using drafting tools, then two parallel lines. I produced ink studies like *Geometric Series in Base 3* and *Visual and Mathematical Matrix* in this context. [Figs. 63 and 64] We were expected to master each task before we moved on. Perspective wasn't introduced until the fourth year. We also took two years of drawing classes that began with still life and moved on to the human body, and finally to sketching landscapes.

In the second and third years, the architecture studio focused on materials and construction. There was a semester of brick, then a semester of wood frame, then steel, then reinforced concrete. In each case the focus was on the inherent qualities and different applications of materials. There was also a course called "Visual Training," a sequence of exercises created by Walter Peterhans, who came to Chicago from the Bauhaus with Mies. The exercises dealt with composition, texture and color, and proportion. In both the drawing and collage studies, the composition of the field (a 20-by-30-inch Strathmore board) was as important as the figure. My *Mass and Voids*, *Planes in Space*, *Warped Planes*, and *Color, Texture, and Their Relationship* belong to this body of studies. [Figs. 65, 66, 67 and 68] The course was so popular that it outlived Peterhans by thirty years!

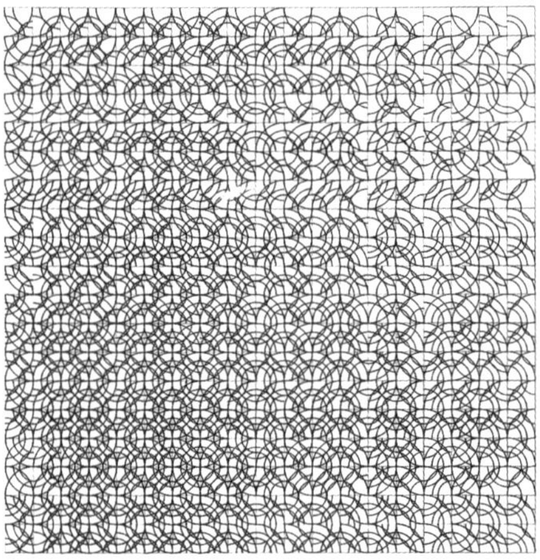

64

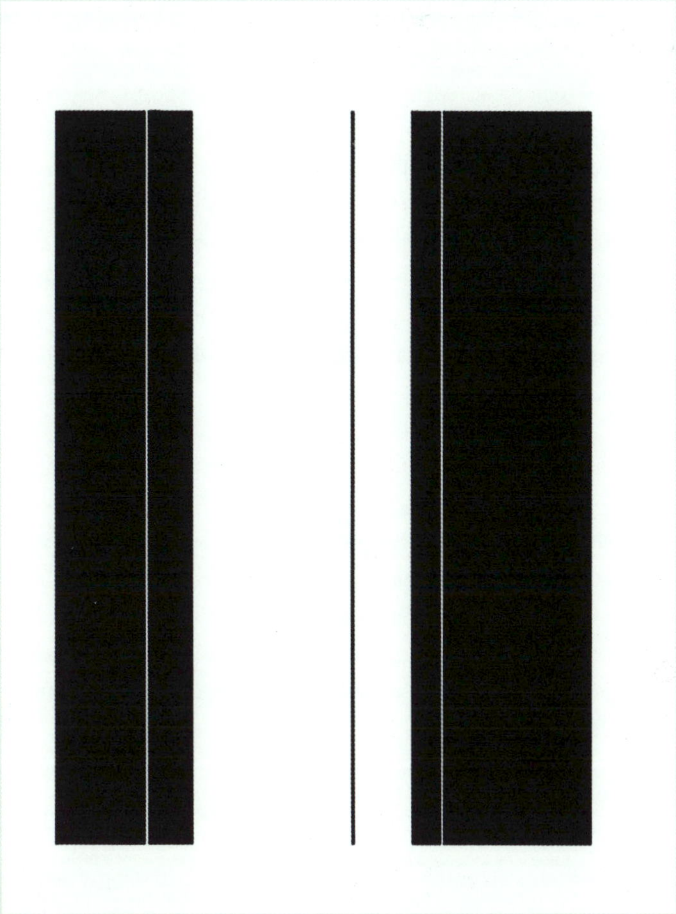

65

66

67

68

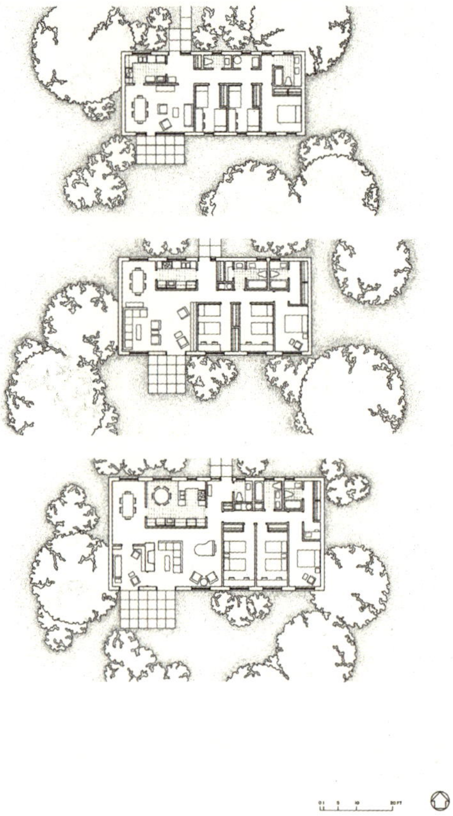

69

In fourth and fifth years, the City and Regional Planning course taught by Ludwig Hilberseimer, who also came over from the Bauhaus with Mies, focused on housing and community development. We started with the simplest components that make a kitchen or a bathroom functional and then added one room at a time to create a house or an apartment. [Fig. 69] I still rely on understandings inspired by these studies with respect to relationships between the human body and architecture, and how relationships between buildings and elements like streets and sidewalks are essential to creating a community.

The curriculum sounds pretty rigid.

Or you could also say thorough! The first time we were asked to work in three dimensions was the fourth-year architecture studio, where the focus was a visual decision-making exercise called "The Space Problem" conceived by Arthur Takeuchi. It remains the strongest experience of my architectural education.

Why was it such a strong experience?

Because it was a synthesis of all I'd learned about both function and aesthetics in the previous three years. It was about understanding space in the abstract – a volume that works at any scale for any type of building. The starting point was a volume – in our case, a 30,000-square-foot space, 18 feet high. We built a model and did various studies within it. [Figs. 71 and 72] The first exercise was to place one wall inside the model to see how, depending on its size and color and position, it would divide the larger space into two smaller spaces. Then we worked with two walls – first in parallel, then perpendicular to one another – to form three spaces.

70

71

72

We would make the walls black and white, long and short, high and low, etc., in order to observe relationships between dimensionality and proportion and their impact on how space would be perceived. Eventually, we introduced different materials or brought in a painting or a piece of sculpture. Then we would study it in collage. [Fig. 70] It was about building intuition.

In the second semester of the fourth year, we were asked choose a site and decide on a program, and then to create a building envelope and the spaces inside. I designed a companion building to Crown Hall, as an expansion for the College of Architecture. [Figs. 73 and 74] My solution referenced Mies's study for his unrealized Library and Administration Building for IIT (1944–45), which would have been one of his greatest works. [Fig. 75] Mies's building had a facade that changed when it turned the corner, a courtyard cut through the center, and a floating mezzanine. [Fig. 76] I worked with the same elements.

73

74

75

That sounds pretty nervy of you.

I was attempting to project what Mies might have proposed thirty years later, trying to channel him. And I was following his master plan for the IIT campus (1939–58).

76

And then you went on to the Graduate School of Design at Harvard.

I worked at Holabird & Root in Chicago the summer of 1983, and went straight from there to the GSD.

Why Harvard?

Three reasons: Myron had just finished teaching a studio there at the invitation of Harry Cobb, who had become chair in 1980. Daniel Libeskind was slated to teach the following semester. And Tod Williams, a fellow Cranbrook graduate and already an architect I admired, recommended it.

What was it like going from IIT to Harvard?

The two schools took vastly different approaches to teaching architecture. At IIT, there were no reviews where students put work up on the walls and everybody talked about it. We just sat at our desks with the instructor, who gave us corrections. The GSD, on the other hand, was about experiencing and expressing diverse and opposing views. And the crits were practically public forums, where alternative voices were consciously sought.

77

How did you fare in that environment?

I felt my IIT training had given me a good foundation, and that I was ready to experience new ideas. I signed up for a studio with Peter Eisenman for the fall semester, back when few people had seen his work. There were eleven of us in the studio. It was all about process, and it was one of the most powerful experiences I've ever had. (And not just because he showed up for the first session with a case of Scotch – one bottle for each week – and told us we had to take turns bringing ice.) He taught us that as architects we control our process, and that more than anything else, the process determines the product: the order in which you ask and answer questions affects the final form of a building. That was an important lesson. But the communication within the studio was probably the most exciting part of it. The term we used most was 'trajectory'. A great amount of effort was put into producing a collective definition of the word. In our definition, it was not only the direction in which something was going, but also the direction from which it had come. In most settings, people understand words quite differently. But in this situation, the goal was to develop a *common* language. It was exhilarating to be totally in sync. After Eisenman, I studied with Daniel Libeskind, who had also taught at the Cranbrook Academy of Art (1978–85). Libeskind's message was about finding your own voice. I found mine in a series of drawings that were architectural in the questions they asked about geometry and measurement, and which simultaneously studied the scale of the building and the scale of the city. [Fig. 77]

Did you also have a job?

In Boston, instead of working at an architecture firm, I took a position as assistant curator at the Institute of Contemporary Art (ICA), where I worked on a major installation of John Hejduk's masques, a sound installation by Brian Eno, and an exhibition on the work of Rodolfo Machado and Jorge Silvetti. The ICA was alive with creatvity at that time. I worked under director David Ross, as well as lead curators Elisabeth Sussman, Gillian Levine, and a young David Joselit. Eventually, however, I was asked to redesign the ICA offices on the top floor of the 19th-century police headquarters at 933 Boylston Street. It was my first professional commission. The museum preparators and I went on to build out the offices ourselves.

How did you get to know Harry Cobb?

Harry knew about my museum work, so he asked me if I wanted to organize an exhibition of work by GSD students under the direction of Chicago architects. It was installed at the Rhona Hoffman Gallery on Superior Street in Chicago during the summer of 1984, between my first and second years. (Years later, I designed Rhona Hoffman's gallery on Peoria Street.) When I returned to the GSD in the fall, the lottery placed me in Frank Gehry's studio. He was working with Claes Oldenburg and Coosje van Bruggen on a camp for children with cancer. But two weeks into the semester Harry asked if I would be interested in working on an independent project with him instead. He knew I had studied with Eisenman and Libeskind and thought it would be interesting to see how their ideas could be applied to a project he was designing for a site at the corner of Market and South 20th streets in Philadelphia, ultimately two 50-story office towers. The 80-story tower I designed was a perfect prism (due to my IIT training), which as it touched the ground fractured and reached out into the landscape (stemming from what I'd learned from Libeskind and Eisenman). [Figs. 78 and 79] There was the purity of the tower in the sky and the complexity of the building's base at the level of the street. Drawing on my two educations, it taught me that different architectures can inform a single project.

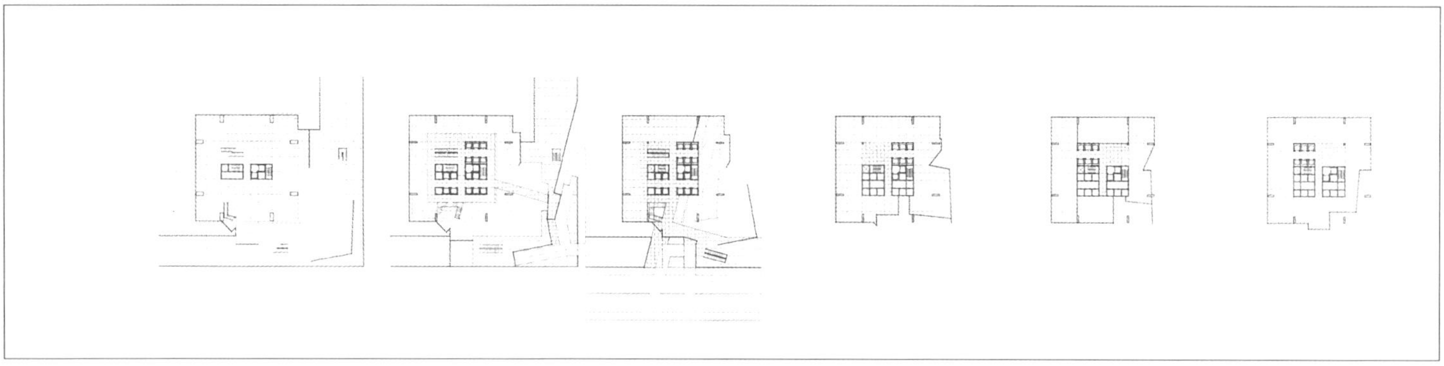

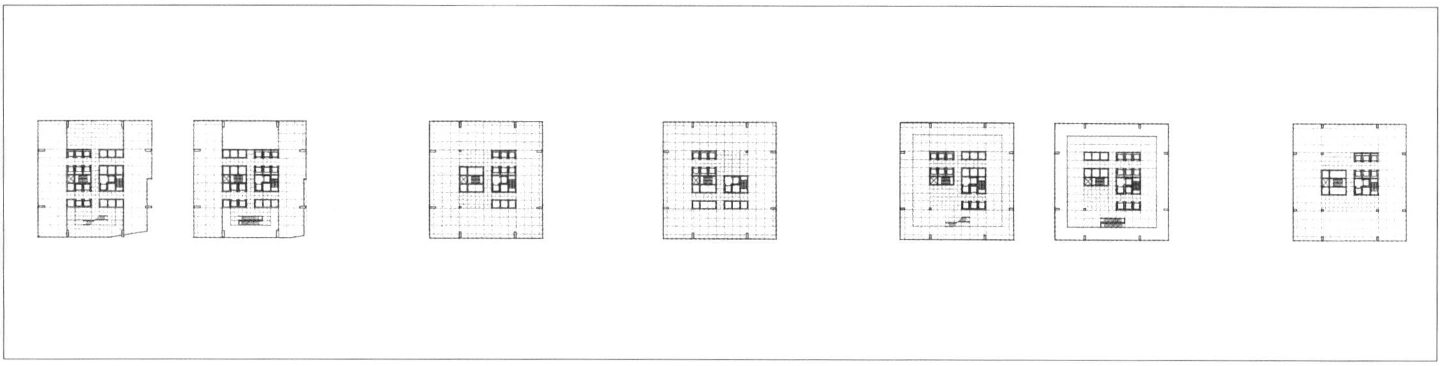

78

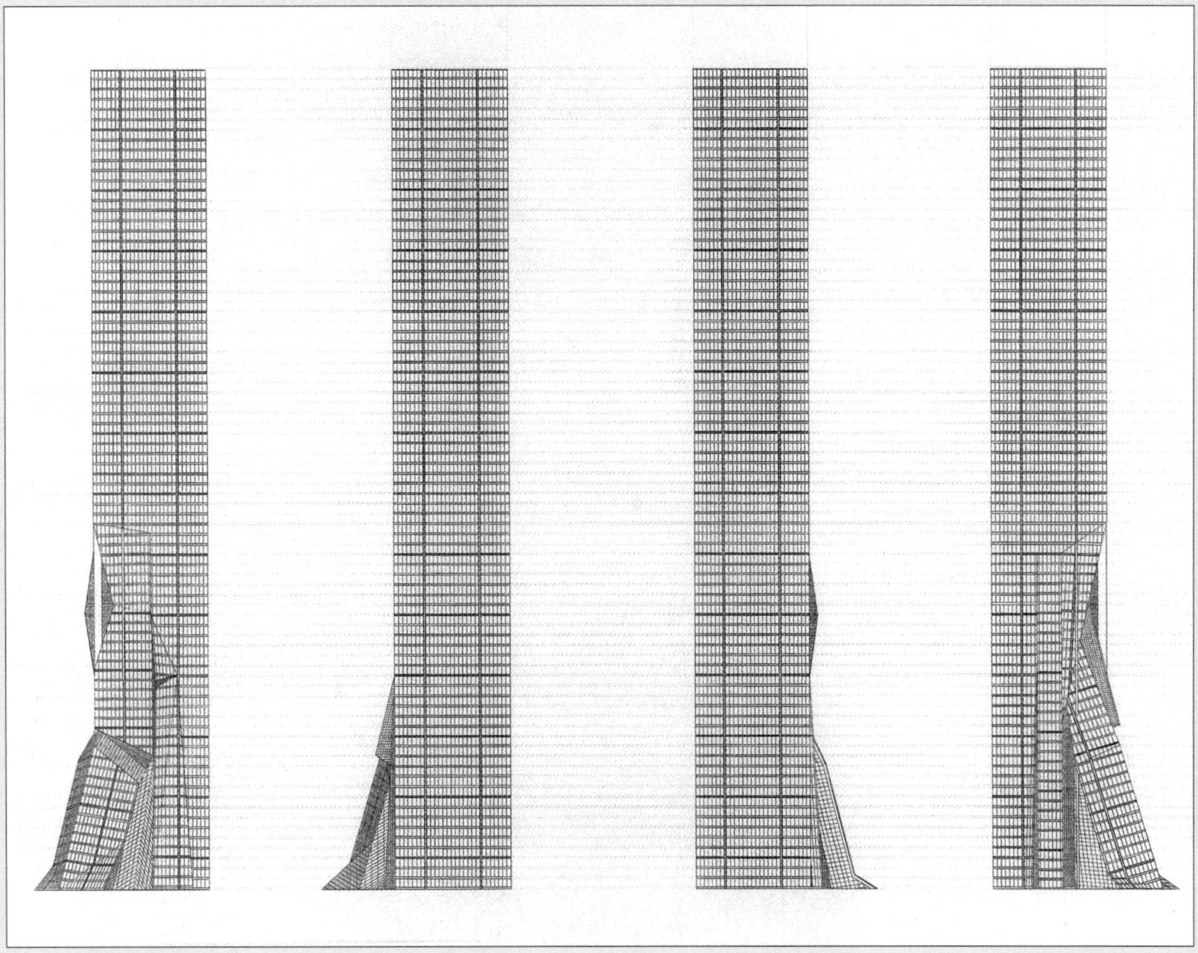

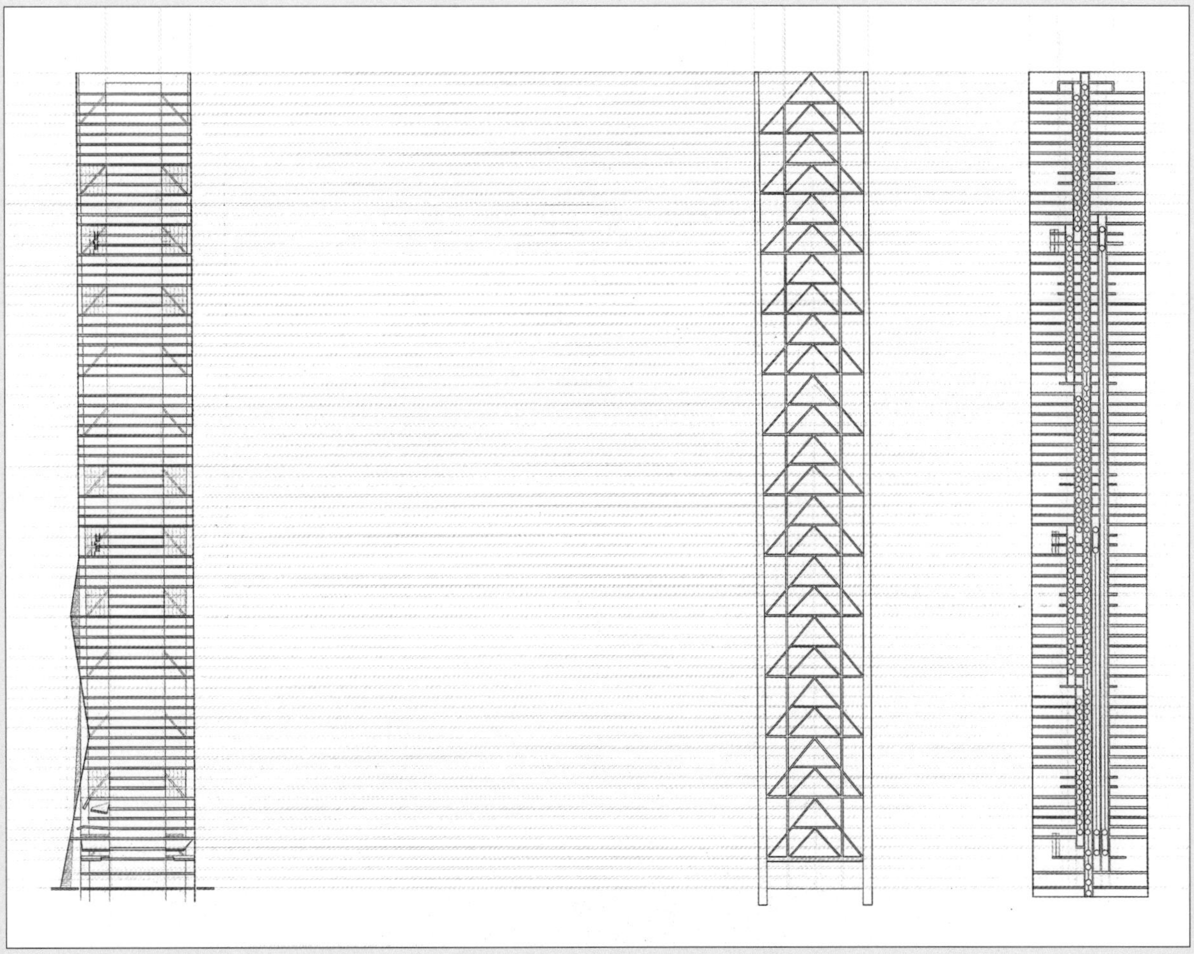

79

What else do you remember about the GSD?

I took a film class in Le Corbusier's Carpenter Center for the Visual Arts (1963), so I was able to spend a lot of time there. [Fig. 80] The strongest element was the ramp, which crosses through the building and deposits you on the other side. It draws you in. You want to be on it, even though you don't know quite where it will take you. If you're an architect, it's something you look at and say, "I want to do that."

80

So far, among your early influences, you've mentioned two Saarinens, both Kahns, Wright, Mies, Cobb, Libeskind, Gehry, Eisenman, Le Corbusier, Goldsmith, Bunshaft, and Yamasaki. That's quite a line-up.

Yes. They all made strong impressions on me, and that was due to their character as much as their buildings. I experienced them as intelligent, articulate, and caring in the largest sense of the word. I didn't just want to do what they did, I wanted to *be* them.

How did you synthesize all those influences?

Eliel Saarinen, particularly at Cranbrook, was about trying to create a richness of experience through complexity; Mies was about simplifying, taking things down to an organizing line or grid. In my own work, I try to do both. The way that plays out, I find, is that there is simplicity in the detailing and complexity in the architectural experience. But after so many years at Cranbrook, where every building was different, not just in style but even in how it related to its site, I know that each project requires a different toolkit and vocabulary.

So you have no one 'look'?

Absolutely not! Each project for me is a chance to create something unique. I'm conscious of the fact that, when you're establishing yourself as an architect, consistency sells. But to me, getting each building right is more important than consistency. My Aunt Robin once took a look at my body of work and said, "At some point, Dirk, you're going to have to choose which one is *your* architecture." The reality is, they're all my architecture!

Westchester

CHANEL
WINDOWS
IMPRESSIONISM
THE ART BOOK
THE LOOM OF ART
French Impressionism

How did you make the transition from school to practice?

From Harvard, I went to work at a small firm in Chicago, Himmel/Bonner Architects (founded 1976), and began teaching studio at IIT. I was also on the search committee that selected Gene Summers to be the new dean of the College of Architecture, Planning and Design. In 1990, Summers asked me to come on full time, as director of the architecture program, which I did. And then, one day, the phone in my office rang. It was a man named Frank Piku. He had seen a model of my IIT project on the piano in my mother's house, and he was taken with it. So, out of the blue, he asked me to design a house for him and his wife Shirley in Michigan.

What kind of clients were they?

Very experienced. They had built four other houses together. In fact, Frank was retiring from his company, which sold musical instruments, and decided to function as the general contractor on the new house. Every day at 7 a.m. he would call me and say, "Okay, what do I do next?" He was my alarm clock! Believe me, it was quite a learning experience, having to guide the contractor, who was also the client, through an unfamiliar process.

What did you learn about the practice of architecture?

I learned that it's not enough to design something great. You have to navigate an enormous process between generating an idea and its realization – a process that begins with gaining the confidence of the client, and includes economics, logistics, and politics.

How did that process play out with the Pikus?

Their only directive was that they wanted a 'distinctive' house. And they wanted it to be white. But I wanted to explore new materials, so I spent a lot of time persuading them to make the house out of lead, which would have been dark grey. When I looked closely at the process of building with lead, I realized we would have had a kind of patchwork surface, and I wanted the building to read as more monolithic.

81

What happened?

Eventually I came back to them and said, "Why don't we make the house white?" And we did. The Pine Lake house in the township of West Bloomfield, Michigan (1991) is white stucco with a stainless steel roof. [Fig. 81]

Were the clients happy in the end?

Yes. Listening to clients, and learning what their lives are about is the heart of my practice. People sometimes say, "Houses are all the same. You just need to know how many bedrooms, how many bathrooms." Nothing could be further from the truth. The challenge of designing houses successfully is that they're never prototypical, never generic. They're individual.

So you're not looking to impose your will on your clients?

The way the client's individuality is reflected in the design is the most important factor in the success of a house. I think I've understood that since I was ten years old, watching Leo Hagan build lower-than-usual kitchen counters for my mother. And then I saw the Smith house by Frank Lloyd Wright, which was so obviously made to measure.

What are some examples of how your houses are 'made to measure'?

I mentioned Frank and Shirley Piku, who were retiring. They talked about loving each other, but still needing separation from one another when they were both working at home. So I consciously created a long path from one home office to the other, and they thanked me for that. [Fig. 82]

You've done other houses for empty nesters.

Yes, and that's not surprising, because many of the houses are manifestations of lifelong wishes – to have access to the woods, or to have a garden in the city, or to live with a view of the ocean or a lake. In many cases, the house is a fruition or realization of a dream.

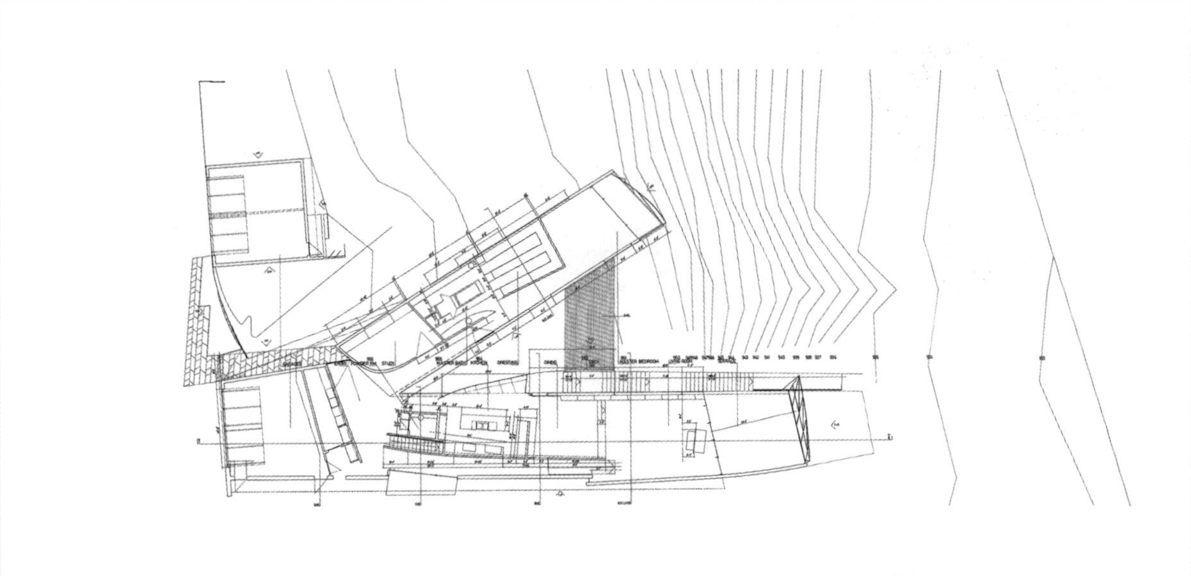

82

The Lake Michigan house is in that category?

Rick and Barbara Silverman wanted a house overlooking Lake Michigan in Winnetka (2015). [Figs. 83 and 84] They wanted their own living space to be manageable in size. But they also wanted rooms for their children and grandchildren, who visit frequently. So we made two houses, one above the other. The upstairs spaces flow. This is Rick and Barbara's private domain, where rooms are open and connected. Downstairs is a series of separate living quarters for the extended family.

83

84

So there's a section to live in and section reserved for guests. Don't all empty-nesters want that?

Not always. Each situation is different. It's important to listen and respond to clients' individual needs. The couple for whom I designed the house in Bannockburn (2011) also have grown children. But those children live nearby, so there was a desire for a large space for entertaining the extended family. The living room and dining room together total almost 2,000 square feet, which is quite unusual. [Fig. 85] Then there is an inner sanctum, private spaces for the clients, with their own personal suite of rooms. [Fig. 86]

85

86

Another couple of empty-nesters are the Bangs, Gary and Kathy, for whom you designed a house on a narrow waterfront lot in Carmel, California. I interviewed them when I was writing an article on compact houses. Kathy told me that when she and Gary met, after both their spouses had died, they owned four homes. She had a 3,000-square-foot condo in Chicago and a 5,000-square-foot house in the Blue Ridge Mountains with a separate guest house. Gary had a 4,000-square-foot house in Alameda and a weekend house in Carmel. They hired you to renovate the house in Carmel. When it was completed, they liked it so much that they decided to live there full-time and started shedding all the other properties.

It's true that they went from houses that totaled 15,000 square feet on 150 acres to 1,800 square feet on a tenth of an acre, and because of zoning regulations in Carmel, we couldn't add so much as a square inch to the weekend house that we renovated (2008). On the other hand, Kathy said, "Now that we're living in the house that Dirk designed for us, we wouldn't want to add to it."

87

How did you achieve so much in so little square footage?

The central feature of the house is a semi-enclosed courtyard that connects physically and visually to all the other spaces, allowing their bedroom, office, and living room to feel much more expansive than they are. [Fig. 87] Depending on which doors are open or closed, the courtyard can be an extension of one room or another. And each space is planned around its essentials.

Kathy said, "The house is perfect for us. It's not a lot of space, but it's the right space." Is that the best thing a client could say to an architect?

It's gratifying to hear that. I have had the amazing good fortune to become friends with the people I have made houses for. And they have given me a gift: the knowledge that my ideas, which are about supporting their choices about how they want to live, have fulfilled their wishes. I hear stories of comfort and beauty, of spaces that change with the light and weather, and travelers coming home to wonder why they ever wanted to leave.

Bucktown

uhaus
HOUSES
SONY
WILLIE NELSON
MOBY DICK
ROCK THE SHACK

Some of your clients, of course, have children living with them. Your house in Marin County, with its white steel I-beams enclosing an interior courtyard, is very Miesian. In fact, it reminds me of the Farnsworth house turned inside out – a glass box with nature in the middle.

Yes, the Marin house (2004) demonstrates the flexibility of Mies's systems. [Fig. 88]

But Mies wasn't known for tailoring his spaces to his clients' needs. You are.

Yes, and in Marin, the needs were quite specific. The clients' son Max was born with cerebral palsy. His legs don't support him. Outside the house he uses a wheelchair, but when he is at home, he pulls himself across the floor. That meant the ground plane had to be completely level, without so much as a threshold to disrupt his passage throughout the house. We even made the front entrance threshold-less, in a part of California where it rains, which required installing a catch-basin below the paving. And in plan, I placed the entry in the middle of the house, so it would be close to the rooms where

88

89

Max would be spending most of his time. There were other considerations, as well. One was making the windows come all the way down to the floor so that Max could see the gardens. [Fig. 89] Another was providing built-in furniture, since he can pull himself onto a banquette more easily than onto a freestanding chair.

It sounds like Max's needs and your aesthetic choices were compatible.

Yes. Mies's notion of 'universal space' and Max's need for 'universal access' were perfectly aligned. Max's bedroom and bathroom have special accessible features, but those rooms aren't much different from the rest of the house, which is essentially defined as barrier-free.

And yet you've never done another house like it.

Each client is different; the architecture necessarily reflects those differences.

There's another house that is very child-centric.

Yes, the house in Wilmette (2010). The clients have three small children, and the wife is particularly committed to education. From the very beginning, she spoke about wanting a space where all five family members would have individual desks as well as a shared table for projects. That really drove the idea of the skylit upstairs space in the middle of the house, which serves as a multi-generational home office. [Figs. 90 and 91]

90

91

The Westchester house is also a family house, but it's organized quite differently.

Yes, the house I designed in Pound Ridge for Charles and Kerry Wilson (2003). [Fig. 92] They were city dwellers who decided to move to the woods – a place where they can literally go out and walk for hours and not run into anyone. They wanted to have their kids grow up in that environment. But inside the house, they wanted clearly defined rooms – not the flowing spaces you see in, say, the Lake Michigan house. It's a bit more formal.

92

Except where it's not.

True, there are also two screened porches, one off the living room and one off the dining room, and Charles essentially lives out there, from the first moment of spring until the last moment of fall, communing with nature. [Figs. 93 and 94] There's also a wonderful sleeping porch upstairs.

93

94

And then there's the house in an industrial neighborhood in Chicago, which is also a family home.

Yes, the Bucktown house (2013) is unusual because it's on a rail line next to an expressway. [Fig. 95] The existing building was a sculptor's studio designed by Harry Weese in the 1970s. In a postmodernist moment, Weese was very mannerist in his use of the square as a motif. He made important contributions to the city, including the Metropolitan Correctional Center (1975), a concrete triangle in the South Loop, and the Seventeenth Church of Christ, Scientist (1968), also in The Loop, on East Wacker Drive at Wabash Avenue. I was asked to add a kitchen, a home office, and a master bedroom to the original studio. The challenge of working with an existing building, especially one with such strong bones, was deciding whether to reject or accept the given architectural language, that is, to extend his idiom or to introduce another. We chose the former approach. If you look at my addition, you'll see that the square is the driver, down to the windows and the module for the masonry. The addition appears to be one and the same with the original building.

95

How did you position the addition on the site?

The original building was positioned at the back of the site, on an alley. We were asked to double it. Instead of putting the addition in the middle of the property, we placed it off to the side. This allowed for a single large yard, more like what you'd have in a rural setting than an urban one. In a way, the siting is a critique of suburban norms, where houses sit in the middle of a parcel, with a functional backyard and a mostly ornamental front yard. It's nicer to have one big piece of land that can accommodate an entry sequence leading through a garden, which not many urban or suburban houses have.

There's the one 'house' no one lives in – the pool house in the rural Midwest. How did that project come about?

The Midwest pool house (2012) started with an existing 1920s structure, which I restored and added to. The addition overlooked a meadow. After a number of years the clients asked me to design a pool house at the other end of the meadow. [Fig. 96] It was far enough from the main house that it became a destination. The owners would go down there to spend the day. Other family members live nearby, so it also becomes common ground. It's the draw, the hangout. It ends up being used by family and friends, and sometimes for informal business meetings. If it had been closer to the house, none of those things would happen as naturally.

How does the pool house relate, architecturally, to the 1920s house that you enlarged?

I had used wood for the addition to the main house, wrapping it in timber colonnades. To tie the buildings together, I used the same material for the pool house – it's wood and glass, not steel and glass. Though the timber itself is heavy, we worked to keep the building profile thin. The roof is supported by a series of cables hung from a kingpost, which allows it to be thinner and more delicate than it otherwise would have been. To further that theme of lightness, the ceiling inside is a plastic membrane tightened around a frame. The membrane is lit from above, which creates a diaphanous surface overhead. It is something like a James Turrell sculpture, in that you don't know what is surface and what is light.

96

And then there's a house that's home to hundreds of living things.

97

Yes, the Oz Park house (2011) in Lincoln Park. [Figs. 97 and 98] The clients interviewed thirteen architects. But one of the things that came out in my interview was that they lived with a number of large fish tanks, and they wanted to make tanks an even bigger feature of the new house. I talked about the tanks I had in my room as a child, how important they were to me, and we bonded over something that might sound secondary, but wasn't.

Some of your houses are very private, given their natural settings or added landscaping, but this one faces a busy street.

Yes, Oz Park is very exposed, and that was part of the discussion with the clients from the very beginning. They were conscious of wanting to be connected to their surroundings, and were comfortable with that.

They were also interested in being 'green' – but this is a very large house.

A commitment to sustainability was one more commonality I had with the clients. So, for example, we didn't just install geothermal wells for heating and cooling; we spent a long time learning how to make their particular geothermal system as efficient as possible. Working together, we secured the first green permit for a house in the city of Chicago. It was also the first time the city had approved putting geothermal wells under the sidewalk in front of a house. As a result – and this was a side-benefit – the sidewalks melt the snow all winter long. The client never has to shovel, and the neighbors benefit as well. It's true that it is a large house, but it's a house that is very well used, and the elements that went into it all meet the most rigorous standards of sustainability. Its high-efficiency building systems, high-performance skin, and 'responsible materials' allowed me to establish a new standard of practice in my office.

98

Bannockburn

It sounds like you learn a lot doing these houses.

One benefit of having worked for such a diverse group of people is that I learn different things from each of them, and that enriches the process with future clients.

Once you have a client and a program, how do you begin to develop the basic form of a house?

In preliminary studies, I test whether a project works better as a gesture, a kind of sculptural insertion in the landscape, or if it needs the control of a measured geometry. I explore both, and see which is more successful at accomplishing our goals.

Tell me what you mean by a 'gesture'.

I mean a house with a fundamentally linear arrangement of spaces that can be twisted or folded or curved.

Can you give an example?

Pine Lake, my first house, designed for the Pikus, started with the desire for every room to have a view of the water. Looking at the natural arrangement of the rooms, in which the living room wants to be next to the dining room, the dining room wants to be next to the kitchen, and so on, led to a strong linear arrangement of spaces, resulting in a long, narrow building. But there was a limit to how long the building could be. The lakefront site was pressed in by neighbors on both sides, which led to the big gesture, folding the house into the site in the middle, in a V. [Fig. 99] The inner side of the V faces the lake.

99

Every room has a water view. On the opposite side, the outside of the fold, we planted a grove of trees, but there's a busy street nearby. So there are very few windows, for the sake of privacy. However there is more to folding a house than simply drawing an angle on the plan. When you fold a piece of paper, it's very different on the inside of the fold than on the outside. The inside of the fold is very tight, whereas the outside is more fractured. The outside sort of frays. With Pine Lake, that fraying made room for the front door, placed to take advantage of the fracture. The inside, on the other hand, is very crisp, a point where the two large sheets of glass, one in each wing of the house, meet at an acute angle of 28 degrees.

What are some other 'gestures'?

The Westchester house is also based on a gesture, though a less obvious one, because the building is rectangular. [Fig. 100] It was not unlike the underlying idea for Pine Lake: to create a narrow building so that every room has a view to the water in one direction and, in this case, a view to the woods in the other. But instead of bending the building in plan, we essentially bent it in section, creating two levels, one sliding across the other. Once that gesture was established, it made sense to make the first floor, which contains the public rooms, more open to outside, and to make the second floor, with all the bedrooms, more private. The bedrooms are sequestered behind wood screens, which give the house its character.

100

And the Lake Michigan house?

Yes, this also developed as a gesture, the idea of 'arms' holding onto the cliff. [Fig. 101] The result is a U-shaped house that cantilevers out over the lake while its 'arms' – almost paradoxically – protect the land behind it. Lake Michigan, by the way, could have been a V-shaped house, like Pine Lake. But the clients said they were uncomfortable with a sharp angle, that they preferred the softness of a curve. And so it became my first house to use curves so prominently.

101

So Pine Lake and Lake Michigan, which were built more than twenty years apart, have a lot in common?

Yes, but they are opposites in their basic orientation to the water, because Lake Michigan is practically an ocean, with waves and storms, whereas Pine Lake is much smaller, more like a suburban pond. What the two houses do have in common is that, because they're both essentially V shapes, they're literally self-reflective. Wherever you are, you are conscious of the architecture. [Fig. 102] This contributes to a richness, a layering of experiences that I try to achieve whenever possible.

How do you organize spaces in a gestural house?

The gesture creates a strong, clear envelope; the goal then is to place objects and materials in that envelope in ways that define and differentiate spaces. Which is very different from the way the exterior walls define the interior spaces of, say, the Marin house. In that case, there is no separation between the shell and the interior.

What approach did you take at the Lake Michigan house?

On the upper level, occupied by the Silvermans, the interior walls have a number of different relationships with the skin of the house; they're constantly moving in and out of proximity to the building enclosure. On the lower level, where there is a need for separation between the rooms, the interior walls are arranged in a radial pattern.

102

How do gestural houses work with their surroundings?

I see the gestural houses as objects set into the landscape, and therefore my inclination is to allow the landscape to develop as if it preceded the house on the land. The landscape doesn't make many concessions to the presence of the house.

So how do you find the entrance?

Kenneth Frampton, when he's evaluating a building, often says, "Where's the door? I want to see the door." I approached Pine Lake as well as the other gestural houses very differently. At Pine Lake, there is a Corten Steel wall along the street inspired by Richard Serra. [Fig. 103] You walk through a gate to what I call the secret garden, a grove of birch trees, which you move through to discover the front door.

103

The Lake Michigan house has no street presence. You make your way down a long drive and come upon the house as you would come upon a sculpture in a park. [Fig. 104] During your journey, the outstretched arms are almost beckoning you into the courtyard. And then, because the courtyard steps down to the lower level, you begin to understand the predicament of the house – that the house is on a precipice and the land is dropping away, something you were not aware of when you first arrived at the front gate. The whole sequence of experiences is about discovery, like walking through the woods at Cranbrook, or looking for the entrance to Frank Lloyd Wright's Smith house.

How do you perceive the landscape from the inside?

From nearly every point inside, you are aware of the landscape, which is private, and Lake Michigan, which is expansive. Even on the lower level – you are constantly experiencing both. You feel both protected and exposed.

And light is coming in from both directions?

Yes, because the landscape steps down the hill, even the lower level gets light from two directions. You never feel like you're underground. It's the lesson I learned from Gunnar Birkerts, when I visited his Library Addition (1981) for the Law School at the University of Michigan.

104

We've talked a lot about the gestural houses. What about the others?

There is a series of houses where I work off a measured rhythm. I start with the site plan, and mark off an area that approximates the size of the house we're going to build. Then I begin to impose a rhythm – which relates to the drawing exercises I did at IIT, as well as the series of drawings I did when I was studying with Daniel Libeskind at Harvard. The measured rhythm serves the goal of alignment, which for me is a key to the modernist vocabulary. When things align, the eye understands them intuitively. Alignment brings order to a space, and when you take that alignment into three dimensions you produce a structure that is comfortable to be in. The mind craves order.

What do you do next?

Once I've established the grid, I begin overlaying the elements of the house. The 'opportunities' created by the grid correspond to how large certain things are in plan. Some things tend to be 6 inches, like a wall, or 2 feet, like a countertop, or 4 feet, like a hallway. That goes back to the space studies that were part of my training at IIT. The grid serves as a template for decision-making, allowing each component to find its best placement.

This seems to describe the Marin house.

If Pine Lake was the inception of the gesture, Marin is where I really explored the grid.

How so?

The physical form of the Marin house comes from a process I developed at Harvard. It starts with defining measuring systems on the x and y axes, which generates a grid, a two-dimensional plan, onto which the necessary architectural elements are placed. Once you've done that, you add perspective, which allows you to create space and form in three dimensions. For Marin, I used a 1212 rhythm along the north-south axis and a 1234 1234 rhythm along the east-west axis. The resulting grid was expressed in a series of drawings. [Fig. 105]

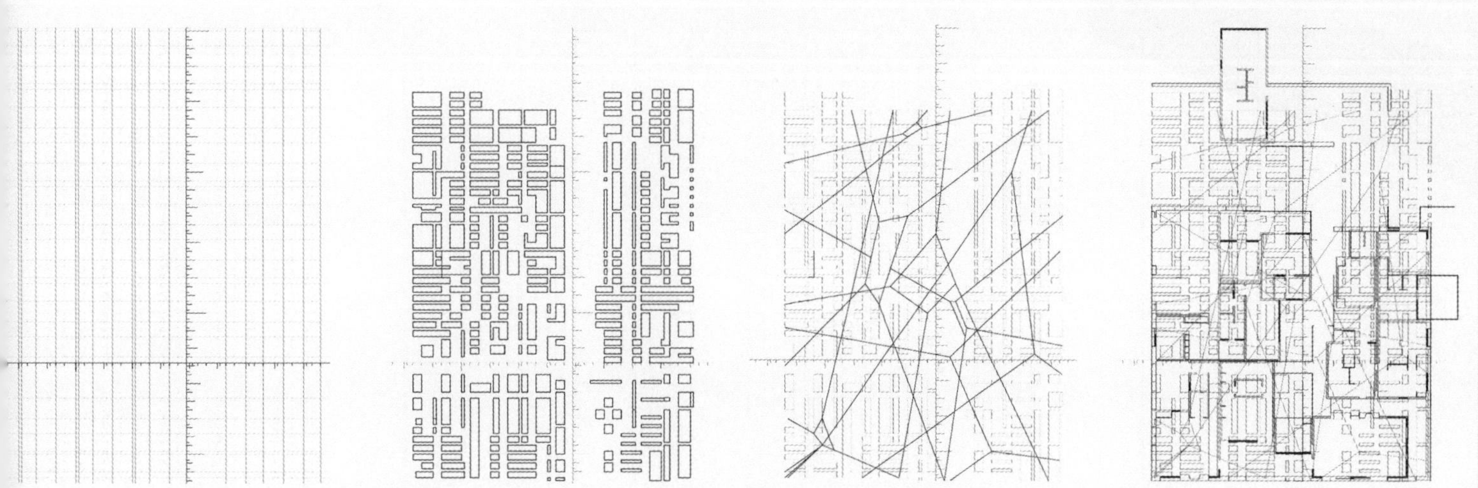

How did the folded roof planes come about?

The tricky thing about grids is the third dimension: How do you make a gridded plan three-dimensional without the building being simply an extrusion? To answer that, I employed perspective, which is, of course, a drawing convention for mediating between two and three dimensions, and overlaid it on what I call the 'frame' and the 'cage'. The 'frame' generated the plan and the 'cage' helped determine the arrangement of spaces, but the 'labyrinth', the overlay of perspective, generated a folded and punctured roof plane. [Fig. 106] The relationship between the planes creates opportunities to vary the volume of the spaces and the way light enters, whether refracted or reflected, direct or indirect, artificial or natural.

106

Midwest

How did you develop this construct?

It was an attempt to reconcile my Miesian training at IIT, which stressed the beauty of rational efficiency, with the new ideas I encountered at Harvard.

Was the Marin house difficult to build?

Actually, the strict grid made the contractor happy. Everything had a precise position. If something was out of place, he knew it instantly.

What was your next 'grid' house?

Five years after Marin, I began designing the Oz Park house. [Fig. 107] Whereas Marin is in a suburban setting, and reaches out horizontally, Oz Park is in the city, and reaches up vertically. So I extended the grid into three dimensions. Remember, in Marin, the grid itself was only two-dimensional; the third dimension was perspectival. Here, there are three axes, three sets of organizing lines, instead of two. That creates structure within which the landscape can push and pull and invade the living space, and the living space can push and pull and invade the landscape.

107

How do you involve the clients in this process?

I start by presenting options to the clients. Sharing different directions that a project might take lets them get involved in a decision-making process that is comparative, based on actual possibilities. The process is essentially the same at the beginning, when we're talking about the placement of the house on the site, as at the end, when we may be choosing a single final piece of hardware.

Can you give an example of how a project developed in dialogue with the clients?

The Bannockburn house illustrates this process. We started by looking at the needs of the clients, a couple with grown children. As I mentioned earlier, the children lived nearby, so the clients didn't need a lot of guest rooms. But they did want a large communal space for family gatherings. We spent years working together to choose just the right site. The property we chose was L-shaped; one leg was long and narrow and the other was almost square. Both had street frontage, so we could have come in from either direction. I started looking at how the building could be positioned to take advantage of both portions of the site. The option we decided on was to place the house at their intersection and run the driveway along the narrower leg. This meant that moving from the street to the house – which would start out as a relatively small object in the distance – would be a rich experience, and that the 'square' leg, which would be behind the house, would provide expansive views of the prairie.

How did you decide on the shape of the building itself?

We explored four basic schemes. One was clearly a gesture, that is, a kind of sculptural form. The other three were orthogonal, based on the intersections of perpendicular lines derived from the outline of the site.

Can you describe those options?

In the gestural plan, the house seems to open its arms to visitors. [Fig. 108] Curved forms reach out into the landscape and at the same time define two different outdoor spaces, one more public and one more private. The forms pull away from one another in the middle, creating a kind of void that serves as the main point of entry. The second plan is based on a measured geometry, but this time the layout is a sort of pinwheel. [Fig. 109] The roofs are angled and intersect at their highest points, forming a cathedral-ceilinged living room. The third plan is perhaps easiest to understand. This one is linear, with rooms arrayed along a spine. [Fig. 110] Conceptually, it's something like the Marin house, where each room is a separate building, with its proportions (including ceiling height) and its relationship to the landscape 'tuned' to its function. The fourth plan, which is also orthogonal, reaches out to welcome you as you come up the driveway. [Fig. 111] Again, it's divided into more public and more private zones that are separated by a pair of reflecting pools. The third body of water is a swimming pool.

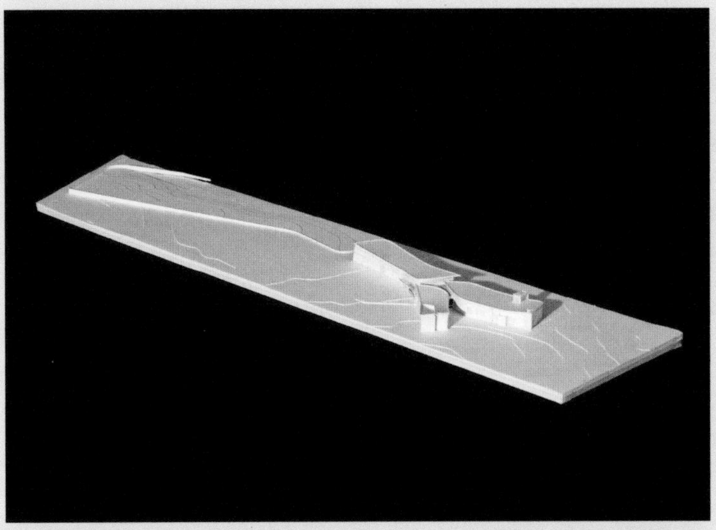

108

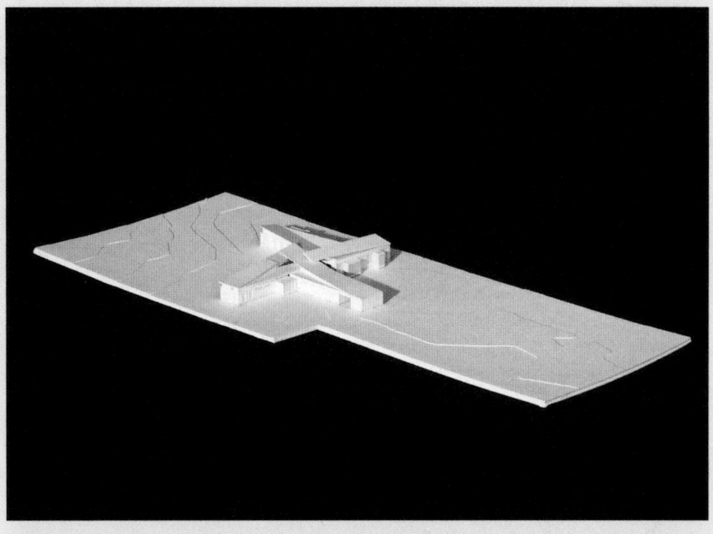

109

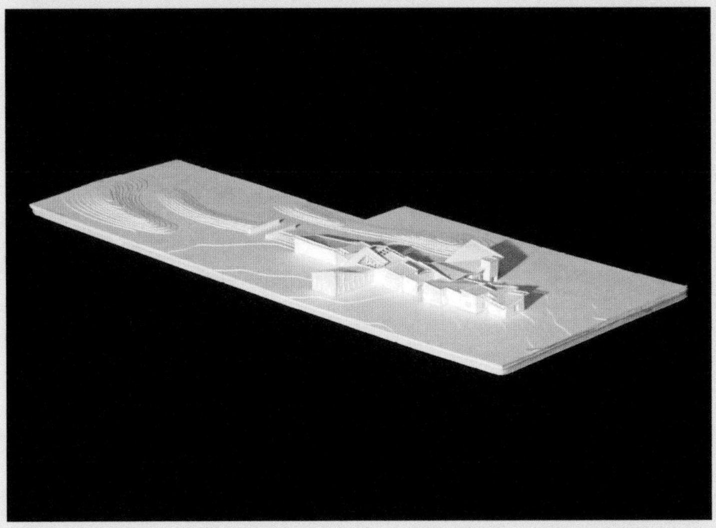

110

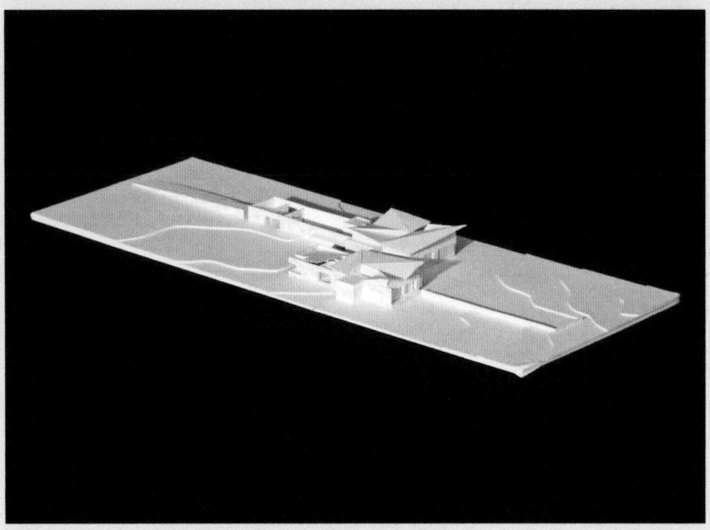

111

Did you develop these consecutively?

No. We presented the four options to the clients at the same time, to give them a sense of the range of possibilities available to them. We showed them the plans and the corresponding paper models. In each case, we talked not just about form but also about function – how each proposal would reflect (and possibly alter) how they lived. For example, if the living room were near the master bedroom, the clients would use it more often than if it were further away. We ended up deciding there should be a 'public' living room for the extended family, and a separate sitting room next to the master bedroom for the clients' personal use.

How did you choose among the four schemes?

There was much discussion about the character of the individual spaces in each scheme, how they related to one another, and how they all related to the site. Eventually, we settled on the fourth scheme. Over time, we dispensed with the water features and the two reflecting pools became gardens, but otherwise, the finished house is closely based on the proposal. The entry is at the center, which the clients wanted, and the living room has 180-degree views through large windows that open onto the largest part of the site, offering a feeling of proximity to wide-open spaces.

When do you begin to develop the materials palette?

I don't start off thinking, "I'm going to make a wood room." My inclination is to make a room of a certain scale and a certain character, and then I might bring in wood to achieve that character. But at the outset, along with volume and proportion, I think about light. Light brings space to life.

Tell me about how you use light.

When you're in a space, you notice where the light is coming from. And you sense the quality of that light. Is it a presence in itself, or is it illuminating and defining the presence of other things? How does it interact with materials, with landscape, with art? How many kinds of light are there? Is it direct light or reflected light, refracted or filtered? I try to work with all the possibilities.

So you use all these kinds of light?

Yes, and Marin is the lexicon. There, each room consciously samples different ways of engaging natural light. For example, the living room receives a sort of fractured light, because the ceiling planes are broken, which means light comes in through skylights in different directions at different times of day. In the family room, there's a skylight where the chimney pierces the ceiling and the limestone fireplace acts as a reflector.

You're getting both direct and reflected light.

112

I think about how light will enter the house when I'm placing it on the site. For example, the Pine Lake house is positioned so that the setting sun will penetrate deep into it. [Fig. 112] When it catches the light, the living room fireplace, which is made of onyx, seems to glow from within. In many cases light comes all the way through the house. The Lake Michigan house is especially beautiful at dawn, when the sun shines through the building, illuminating the inner courtyard. Light moving through the house reveals the passage of time.

So far we've only talked about natural light.

It's also important to think about electric light, which determines how the house will be perceived at night. At night, a building can become a kind of lantern. I know how strong that effect can be, because it is a defining feature of Mies's Lake Shore Drive apartment buildings, where I live. At night, the spaces around the bases of the buildings are defined entirely by light. It's a powerful architectural experience.

After light, what's the next thing you think about?

Materials and art and landscape. Those three things bring color, pattern, and texture into the mix. A lot can be achieved by juxtaposing them – not just because of their physical characteristics, but because of what they represent. Materials tell stories of the past, art comments on the present, and landscape holds the promise of the future.

Can you elaborate?

Natural materials, wood and stone, have the history of the planet embedded in them. They have their geologies and their lifelines. By cutting and shaping them, we expose their history. So for me, materials are about the past. Art is the present. It brings an often serious consideration of the state of the world, either celebrating it by making something beautiful, something that represents the highest human achievement, or by analyzing and critiquing it. Landscape is the other end of the temporal spectrum. Landscape is growing and alive, and thus is the embodiment of the future.

Do you take advantage of that temporality?

Yes, and in two different time frames: the seasonal and the life cycle. For this, I've relied on wonderful collaborators, including Andrea Cochran, Maria Smithburg, Doug Hoerr, Mimi McKay, and all the people who work with them to help create landscapes that will look different in six weeks, in six months, in six years. That temporality complements the permanence of the architecture.

You've made clear that landscape isn't an afterthought – it's not just about planting trees after a house is built.

113

Not at all. My design process involves creating ways for landscape and architecture to interact. Indoor space and outdoor space can have complex relationships. With Lake Michigan and Pine Lake, the shape of the buildings defines the outdoor spaces. With the Bannockburn house, the way the wings intersect captures spaces that are within the perimeter of the house but open to the exterior. [Figs. 113]

114

With the Wilmette house, landscape acts as architecture. We brought a row of trees close enough to the face of the house to create an outdoor room, a void between architecture and woods. [Fig. 114] In the case of the Westchester house, I created outdoor spaces by extending the structure beyond the envelope of the building. And for Bucktown, I installed a concrete block wall 12 feet from the house, which defines a large outdoor room with a fireplace and a grill. In Marin, the weave of indoor and outdoor is even finer. Not only is every room its own building, but they're arranged in a way that creates opportunities for landscape to fill the spaces between them. And then Oz Park renders that effect three-dimensional.

So we're not talking about conventional backyards?

All good views have foreground, middle ground, and background. The foreground may be most important, because, in addition to just being what you see from the building, it can actually help shape the building. It's an edge the building pushes up against, and vice versa.

Can you give an example?

I'm looking at a window right now. There is a tree outside the window; several of its leaves are touching the glass. The tree, by its proximity, helps define the room. I don't have to get up and walk to the window to see it. The landscape becomes part of the experience of being in the room.

So landscape is more than gardens you see in the distance?

For me, landscape is not just Olmsted, it's not rolling hills and lawns, like something you look at in a painting. It's about things you can touch.

Is it the influence of the fish tanks you had as a child?

That was certainly a way of seeing nature in close-up. I now have a terrarium in my 26th-floor apartment. [Fig. 115] It's a 4-by-9-foot glass box filled with tropical plants. The effect is very different from just having potted plants sitting in the room. A room with a houseplant in it is still one room. The terrarium subdivides the room. It creates spatial richness.

115

Can you trace this love of nature 'close-up' to the buildings you saw as a child?

Absolutely. Buckminster Fuller's Biosphère at *Expo 67* made me very conscious of the fact that landscape could be contained. But Philip Johnson's de Menil house (1948) really upped the ante. There, the indoor space wraps around the outdoor space, so when you are inside the house, not only are you looking at nature, but nature appears to be pushing its way in. And then there is the Ford Foundation Building, which took my breath away. I remember thinking, they just made a forest inside a building, in the middle of the city. That was a very bold move. There was something very optimistic about it – like the Ford Foundation itself.

And then there was the Farnsworth house.

There, the landscape is the enclosure. But it's essentially middle ground and background – there isn't the proximity of, say, the de Menil house. When I'm at the Farnsworth house, my inclination is to go outside to experience the landscape. A valuable lesson I learned from Farnsworth, and also Crown Hall, where I teach, is the importance of the relationship between the window and the ceiling plane. When there's an opaque vertical surface above the window, your eye stops at the wall, and the landscape beyond becomes a picture in a frame. I like to create the sense that you are in the landscape, not just looking at a picture of it. So I design spaces where the windows touch the ceiling. I recently renovated an apartment overlooking Chicago for a client who had already lived in it for many years. I lowered the ceiling more than a foot to bring it flush with the top of the windows. The client was skeptical, but when he moved back in, he said, "I feel like I have an entirely new view of the city." It's because his eye used to stop at the plane of the window.

Your landscapes are quite varied.

I think it's important to distinguish between two strains of residential landscape design, one involving a 'naturalistic' approach, as if to suggest that the garden predated the architecture, the other extending the geometries of the architecture into the landscape. Westchester is an example of uncultivated landscape, where the house inhabits a pre-existing forest. In Carmel, there were two mature cypress trees that framed the view, so we cradled the building between them. The only landscape we added was a row of bamboo and a moss garden behind the house. A shower sits at the back of the house in a glass box that is transparent near the ground and translucent above, so you see moss through transparent glass from your calves down. Other naturalistic landscapes include the birch grove at Pine Lake and the courtyard garden at Lake Michigan, which both appear to exist independently of the architecture, even if they are bordered by it. I love navigating that kind of irregular landscape, because you don't know exactly how you'll get where you're going.

Like on the paths at Cranbrook?

Yes, you know you're moving toward a destination, but the route isn't immediately apparent.

Where else have you used naturalistic gardens?

At Oz Park, the planted beds are new, and they're relatively small, but they're not geometric. Essentially, they're meant to look as if the seeds blew in. [Fig. 116] I was working with the idea of the captured landscape. The ultimate captured landscape is a terrarium or an aquarium, and the idea was to take that to a larger scale. There is landscape on six different levels. It takes the effect I had explored in earlier projects, that is, giving every room in the house a dynamic relationship with nature, into three dimensions. The house rose five levels, so we simply took the landscape with us.

116

And there's also a relationship to a much larger landscape?

One of the goals was to connect the house to the park across the street. On the main living level, I placed the landscape at a height that lets it connect to the trees across the street, eliminating the street and cars from the view.

At the other extreme, the pool house in the rural Midwest is surrounded by a vast meadow, but you wanted to add foreground and middle ground.

Right. I created a density of landscape around the pool and the pool house.

Oz Park

You added landscape to a site in the middle of what looks like Central Park?

This is a perfect example of the difference between distant landscape that you look at, and proximate landscape you actually live with. I wanted as much proximate landscape as possible, so I wrapped windows around the pool house, which is essentially a summer living room. The bathrooms and changing rooms are windowless, in separate buildings a few feet away. That allowed the living room to inhabit the garden. At Bannockburn, gardens seem to enter the space of the house. In plan, three wings intersect to create outdoor spaces within the building perimeter, making proximate landscape part of the experience of the house. Landscape also separates parts of the house, visually, keeping private rooms private.

But Marin is one of your more ambitious attempts to create proximate landscape.

The way the rooms are organized leaves space for seven interior gardens, and every room has a relationship with one or more of them. The gardens vary considerably in size. Some you can step into, others you can only look at. The geometries of the house and various lines of vision determined their design and the plant materials. Andrea Cochran brilliantly extrapolated from the geometries to a pattern or just stones on the ground, or an element that reaches up to the sky, such as a tree, or something that occupies the middle ground, like a fountain. Each garden was also conceived with an eye to how it would look if you were standing, sitting, lying down, or confined to the floor, like Max.

And where glass showers are surrounded by walled gardens, do they offer enough privacy?

Yes, and for the more minimalist client, there is no need for curtains. [Fig. 117]

117

You've suggested that certain materials have stories to tell.

Each material brings something different, and there's something important in those differences. The growth lines that become figuring in wood, the geology and fossilization that determine the character of a piece of stone – these, to a science nerd like myself, are fascinating stories. Man-made materials also tell stories about their composition and fabrication. Whether it's glass embedded with linen, or terrazzo composed of an aggregate, I choose materials in large measure for the stories they tell. And to emphasize those stories, I try to use materials monolithically so that they can be appreciated in and of themselves.

You also design the furniture for many of your houses.

Clients have given me the opportunity to design furniture, which has been a very enriching component of the practice. It goes back to Cranbrook – the idea that every space should have furniture that's part of the overall aesthetic.

118

But isn't designing a house challenging enough?

In most cases, the reason we design custom furniture is simple: we didn't find something we loved, something specific to the architecture and the place. In addition, designing furniture gives us a chance to investigate what can and can't be done with various materials. Working at the scale of furniture allows us to explore ways of using materials that wouldn't be practical at the scale of a building, and sometimes investigations at that smaller scale produce results I later incorporate into my architecture. For instance, at the moment, we're working on a canopy for an urban rooftop, and I'm looking at different options based on furniture I've designed. The canopy will look like furniture, but at a much larger scale.

119

How do you decide what materials to work with?

Sometimes furniture needs to have a real presence. In the case of a coffee table I designed for an apartment in downtown Chicago, the idea was to create a topography out of layers of stone. [Fig. 118] We simply stacked pieces of marble on top of one another; their weight (and a few metal pins) holds them in place. For the Lake Michigan house, I designed a coffee table made of three pieces that fit together. [Fig. 119] One is quartzite, one is wood, and one is acrylic. The idea was to investigate how a complex form can be created using materials with very different properties.

Not all of your furniture is so heavy.

That's true. For another part of the Lake Michigan house, we created a set of three cast-aluminum sawhorse bases to support a 12-foot-long translucent tabletop. [Fig. 120] The table is positioned in a narrow, bridge-like space, and I wanted it to be as light as possible. We worked with our structural engineer, Paul Endres, to calculate the minimum amount of material necessary to carry the load. The molds were hand shaped, and this is visible in the surface of the metal. Because the table sits on a hard terrazzo floor surrounded by steel and glass, I wanted it to have a soft finish. In fact, sometimes I want the furniture to be light so that it doesn't compete with the architecture. In the case of the Wilmette house, there's a breakfast nook made of wood that has its own presence, its own weight, so I wanted the table to almost float. Its base is aluminum, which is about as light as metal gets. We rolled the sheet aluminum and then milled it to leave as little material as possible. [Fig. 121] I worked with rolled metal again, at a larger scale, in designing a table in brushed stainless steel for an apartment in Washington, D.C. [Fig. 122]

120

121

122

123

What other materials do you use?

For another dining table, I used steel again to fabricate a set of bases in the form of metal 'straps' folded like Mobius strips and then sandblasted – a process that makes the surface glisten. [Fig. 123] The bases can be used one, two, or three at a time. The dining table in the Oz Park house is surrounded by landscape, which was the impetus for its organic shape. [Figs. 124 and 125] Our fabricator's triple-axis milling machine gave us the opportunity to create a honeycomb of wood that resembles a shade tree in section, and using a translucent tabletop allows for the structure to be perceived from above.

How would you characterize the relationship between your architecture and art?

Art is essential to the experiences of my houses. To me, art and design objects express the breadth of human creativity. I collaborate with my clients and artists – each case is unique – to select works for particular spaces. Sometimes, as in the case of a Frank Lloyd Wright house, the architecture leaves no room for art. And sometimes, as in the Farnsworth house, the views rise to the level of art. But for the houses I design, paintings, photographs, and sculpture enrich the experience. So when I begin work on a house, I think about art from the very inception. I conceive of locations that will embrace works of art.

124

125

Are you involved in selecting art for the spaces you design?

I've been fortunate to have clients who are collectors, and in other cases, I'm the one who introduces the subject of art. In each situation, I try to find works that will enrich the space, not only in their appearance, but also in terms of what they communicate. The selection process is a matter of considering the spirit of the house and the character of its occupants.

Which artist have you worked with most often?

Wolfgang Tillmans, whom I came to know in the process of acquiring work for the Art Institute of Chicago. As a photographer, he has at one point or another investigated nearly every application of the medium, including journalism, which is where he started, and urban imagery, nature, and portraiture. He does aerial photographs, and then he does very, very interesting things in the darkroom, where he is working in the trajectory of Man Ray, creating fanciful abstractions on photosensitive paper. These are not images taken through a lens, but they are nonetheless very much photography. Another thing he has contributed to the art of photography is the juxtaposition of images in large-scale installations, which is a very interesting part of his practice. This idea of installation has an obvious connection to architecture. You have to consider space to be able to do what Tillmans does, for example, with *Urgency XXIX* (2006), which I installed in a home in Washington, D.C. [Fig. 126]

126

And Jim Hodges?

Jim's pieces are beautiful. I realize that I haven't used the word beautiful with you yet, but beauty is something that is on my mind all the time. The gold in Jim's work functions as a mirror in such a way that the pieces engage one another in reflection – for example in his piece titled *here it comes* (2009), installed in a Chicago apartment. [Fig. 127] It also matters that Jim is an activist; he focuses on how we can do better in our fragile world. That brings an additional level of meaning to the work.

127

Michele Oka Doner?

Michele was the first artist with whom I collaborated. At Pine Lake, her *Doppler* (1991) became a threshold you crossed when entering the house. It was embedded in the site, both literally and figuratively. [Fig. 128] For the Lake Michigan house, we took the collaboration to another level, asking her to create a centerpiece for the large courtyard. *Telchine* (2013), the fountain she designed, takes the form of a bronze armature resembling coral which appears to be breathing water. [Fig. 129]

128

129

130

And Máximo González?

Máximo's work is about giving value back to things that have been discarded. We worked on one project together for an office in Chicago. His installation *Dream* (2006), a frieze made out of worthless money, told a story about industry and commerce in a provocative and engaging way. [Fig. 130]

Beverly Fishman?

Beverly is artist-in-residence and head of the Painting Department at the Cranbrook Academy of Art, which is where I got to know her. Her *Untitled (Opioid Addiction)* (2015) in the Bucktown house belongs to an unusual body of work, a compelling form of portraiture that uses the iconography of pharmaceuticals to explore relationships between people and their drugs – a very timely subject. [Fig. 131]

131

These are all living artists.

When I see work I like, I take the opportunity to learn about the artist's intent. That's why I tend to look for work by living artists. I meet the artists, and I encourage my clients to meet the artists whenever possible. The work becomes richer with the mutual understanding this engenders.

No exceptions?

Well, I've had a weakness for Harry Bertoia since I first discovered his work while I was studying at Cranbrook.

You hadn't mentioned Bertoia before.

Bertoia studied at Cranbrook. After graduating, he re-established the metal workshop in 1939, and headed what was then called the Metalcrafting department until it was suspended in 1943 due to the wartime shortage of material. His presence was very much felt there, as well as in the Detroit area at large.

What I appreciate is the strength of his compositions, as well as their playfulness. Pieces like his *Untitled (Sonambient)* (ca. 1965) in the Marin house are structured like architecture because they are interactive, but they move, making their own music and engaging multiple senses all at once. [Fig. 132]

Well, it seems like we have come full circle.

Yes, my awareness of Bertoia, like so many other influences, dates to the years at Cranbrook, where my experience of the arts and the work of artists, architects, and landscape designers so strongly shaped what would become my own approach to the work of architecture. For me, making architecture, like life, is goal-oriented and collaboratve, enriching and synergistic, in the sense that each thing that is accomplished resonates beyond the task at hand to inform and inspire the practice at large.

132

Marin

A Note on Drawing

Dirk Denison

There is great pleasure in putting a line down on a surface. The many different kinds of drawings that result – conceptual sketches, freehand studies, hard-lines, plans, elevations, sections, perspectives, and even collages – serve specific goals. Some drawings are expedient, made very rapidly as a means to seize an idea and get it down on paper; other drawings are composed more slowly as a means of testing ideas. The diagrammatic sketches on the cover of this book, for example, are a kind of code I generate to test different options for elaborating the formal parti of a design idea. In the end, all these types of drawings start as a line that we as architects put down with our own hands.

In the conversation that forms the core of this book, I talk about the evolution of my drawing practices, from sneaking moments to sketch on graph paper during math classes at Cranbrook to grappling with Walter Peterhans's rigorous drawing exercises at IIT to exploring purely speculative drawings while studying with Daniel Libeskind at Harvard. All of these contributed to my understanding of drawing's potential to express architectural thinking.

Whereas a concept sketch allows for early testing of an idea, studies and other kinds of drawings become vehicles for understanding the essence and order of an idea and synthesizing all the parts at play in it. Whether freehand or hard-line, architectural drawings have the potential to layer concrete proposals over abstract thought. Rendering the axis of a sight line clear through a plan – as a line with arrowheads at both ends – references the concept of a physical connection to natural light, the out-of-doors, or a view. The ergonomics of space-making can be tested using measurement and scaling of various elements to understand the potential for movement in space and to determine where adjustments need to be made to compensate and regulate.

Different modes are used to test and ground ideas at different stages of the design process: to explore variants, determine solutions, communicate a proposal that engenders the confidence that leads to the realization of an idea, and finally to specify the execution of the idea at the level of construction drawings. The strongest of architectural proposals can fail if the idea is not rendered in terms that convey the architect's thinking to a client. At the other end of the spectrum, a great architectural idea that has been well communicated graphically, can fail at the level of the detail that was not thoroughly worked out in construction drawings.

In particular, architectural site plans – like maps – have the power to demonstrate, illuminate, and make concrete the complexity of a multitude of considerations – condensing the substance of years of conversation and expressing the thinking that occurs in moments of clarity over the course of designing and building a house. Site plans comprise layer upon layer of information – the character of the land, its topography and relation to bodies of water, how storm water runs through it, how it is oriented to the sun, a street grid, or a larger context, how the site is landscaped with trees, hedges, lawns, gardens, and hardscape like paths, patios, courtyards, swimming pools, and ball courts. Layering a detailed floor plan into a site plan reveals how interior spaces are physically and visually connected with exterior spaces by doors, windows, and skylights, in addition to rendering the built spaces and their scale and positioning in relation to one another. Also embedded in these conjoined plans are facts about construction and the materials used to build walls, floors, and cabinetry, as well as locations for furnishings and artworks.

The site plan drawings that follow represent the ten houses profiled in this book in their geographical locations. They are all presented at the same scale and can be read comparatively. These plans are also the final recording of an ardent process of decision-making that has been driven at all stages by the act of drawing.

Lake Michigan 2015

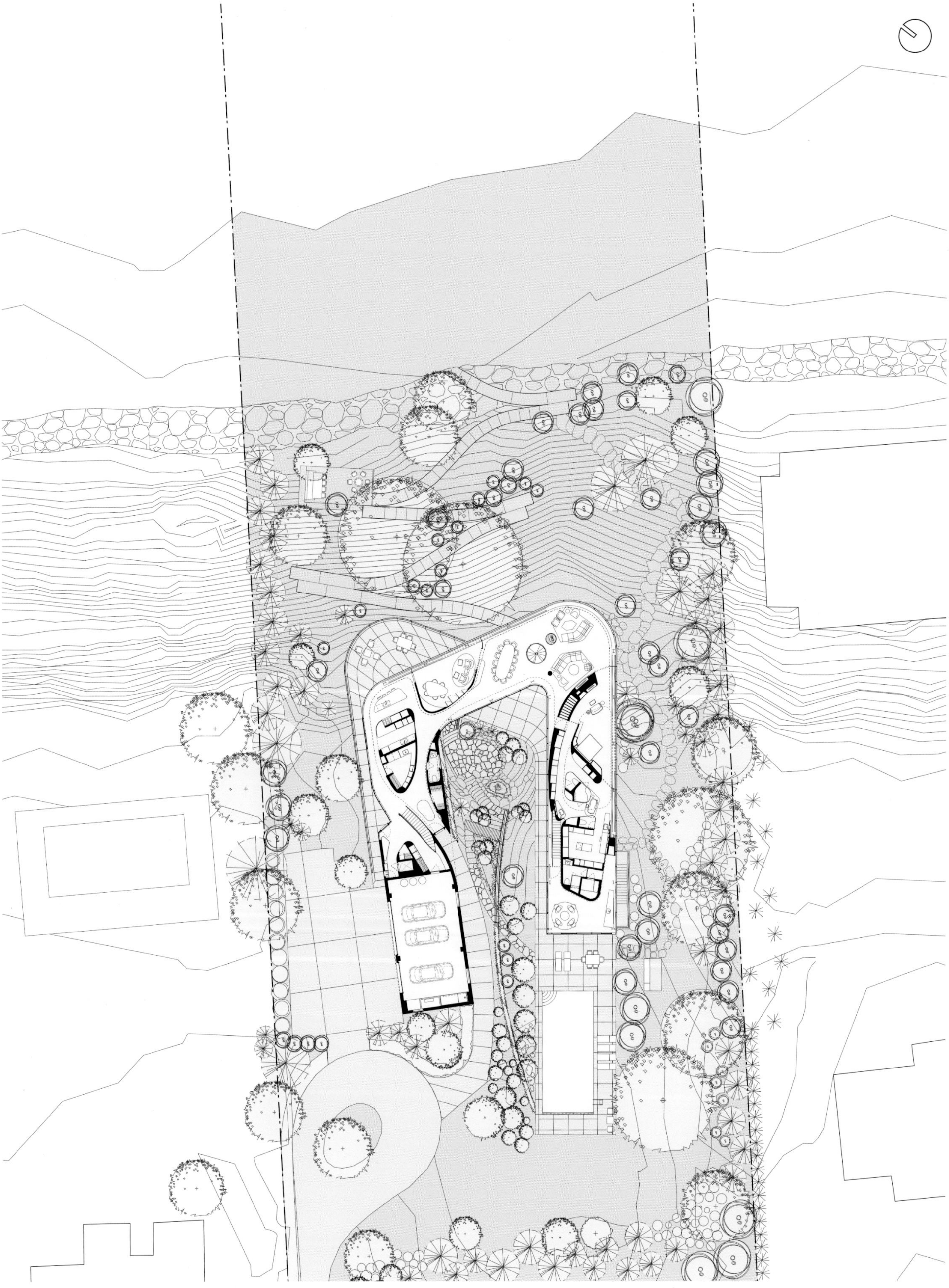

Carmel 2008

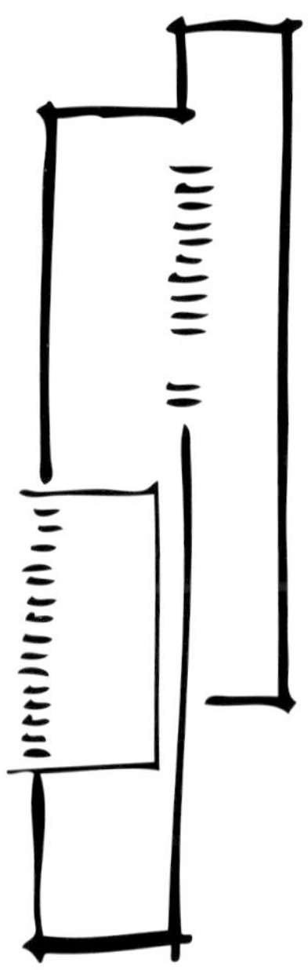

Wilmette 2010

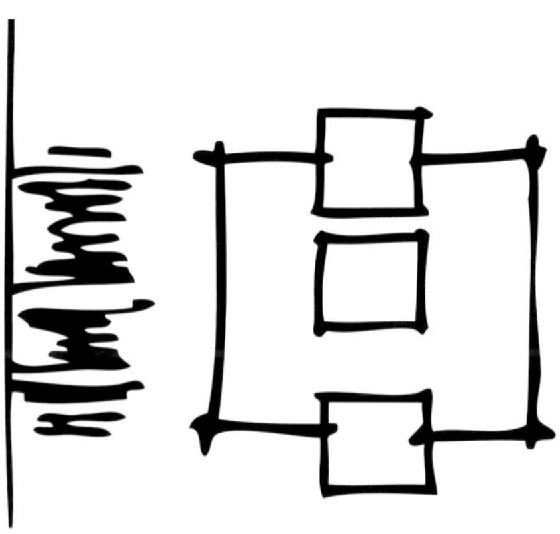

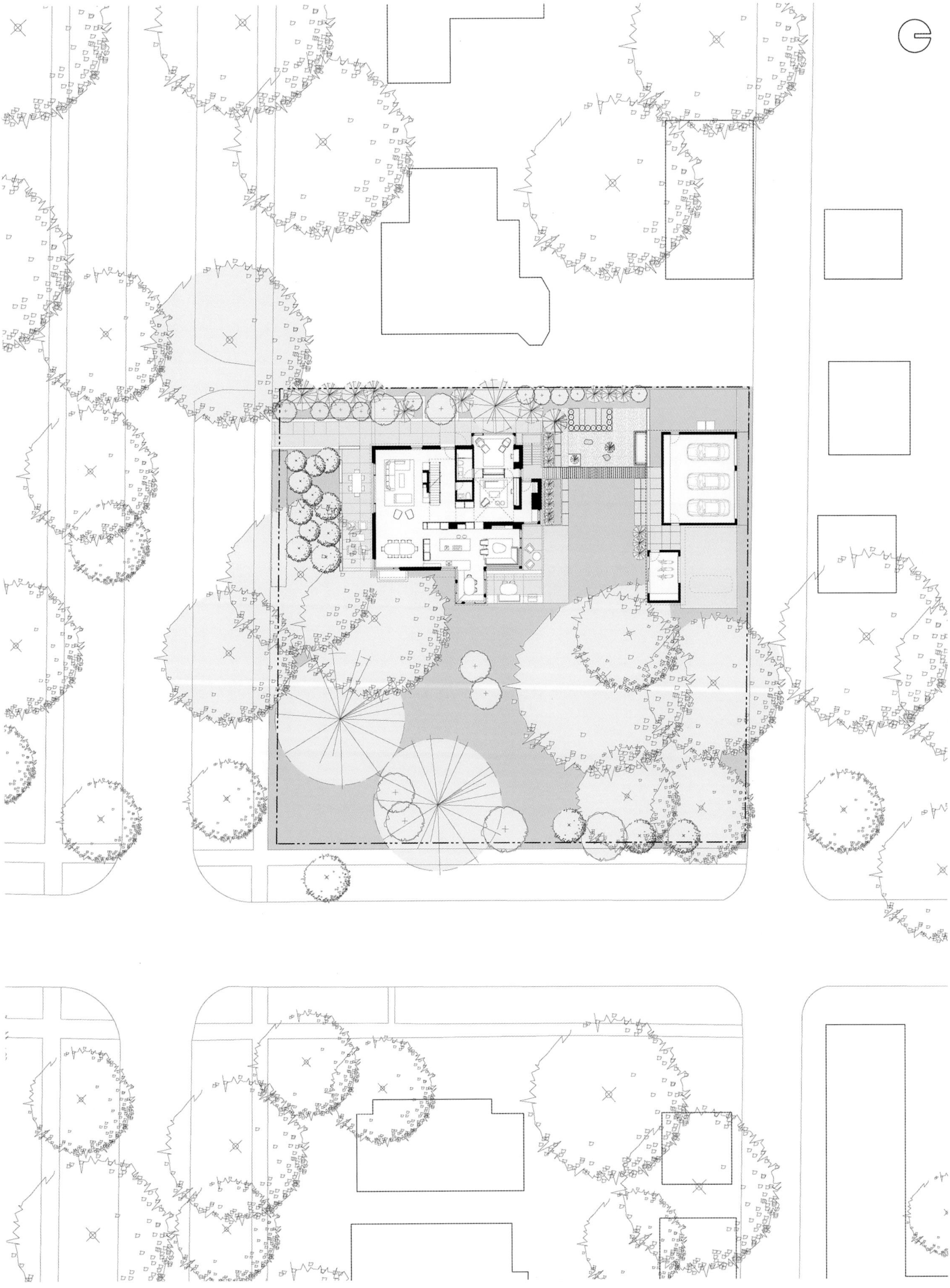

Pine Lake 1991

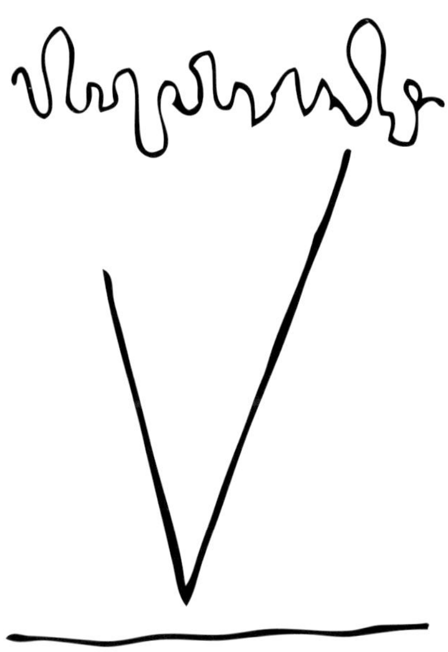

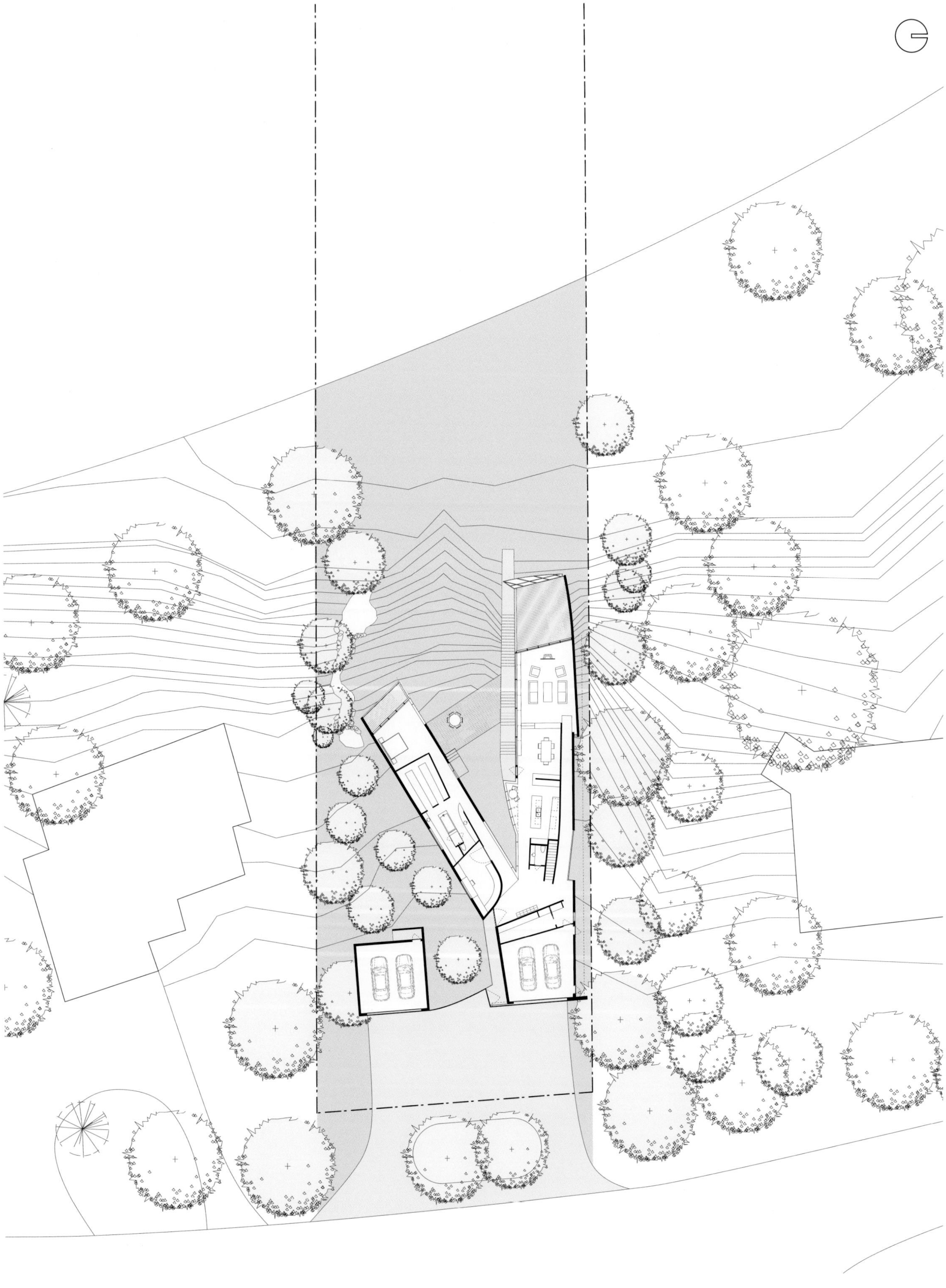

Westchester 2003

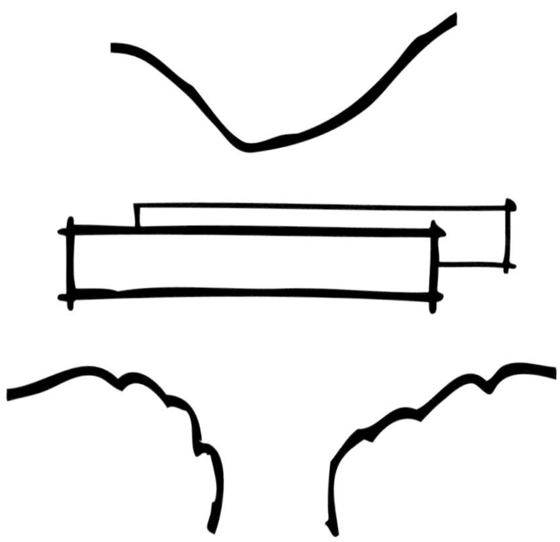

Bucktown 2013

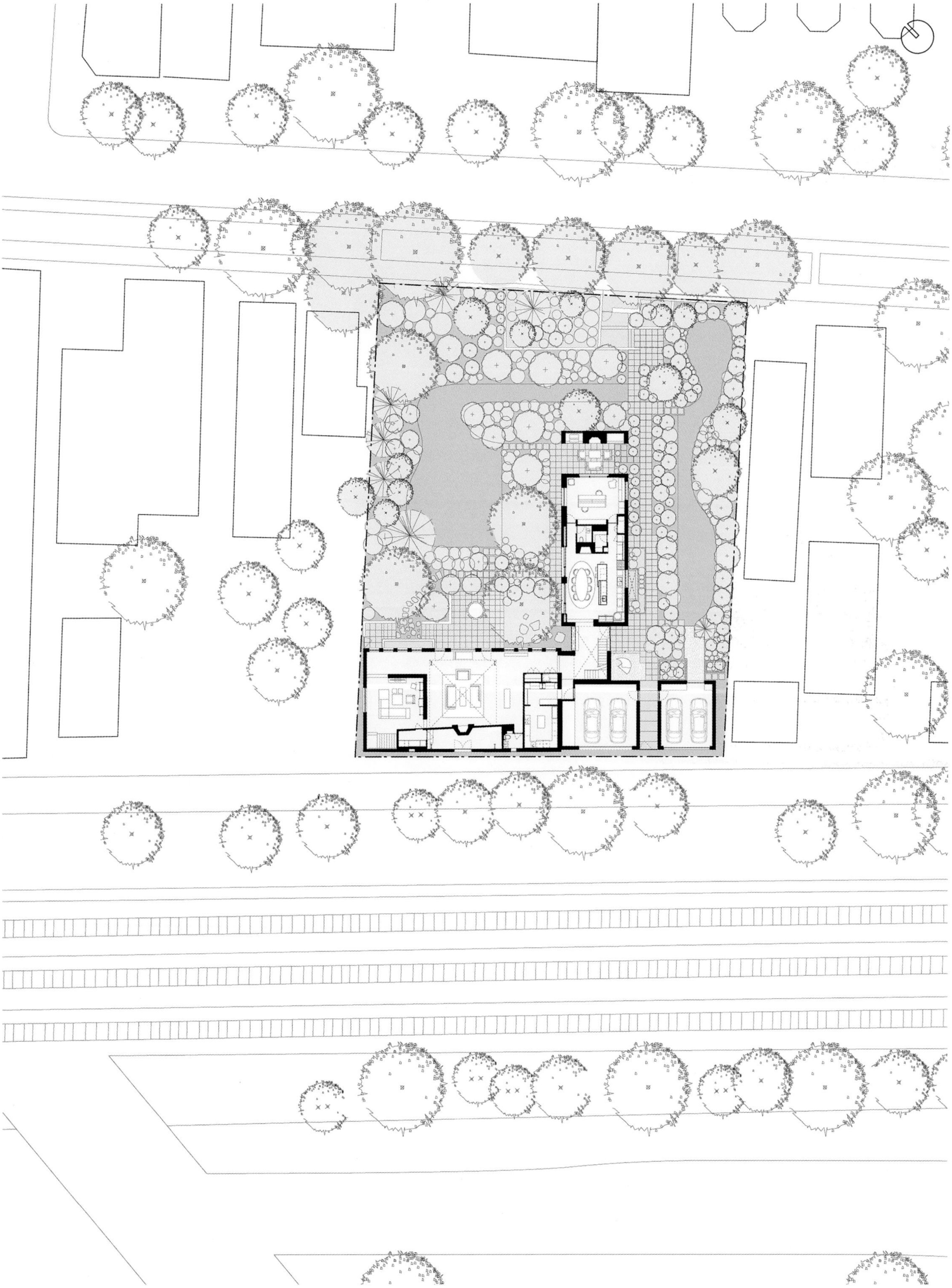

Bannockburn 2011

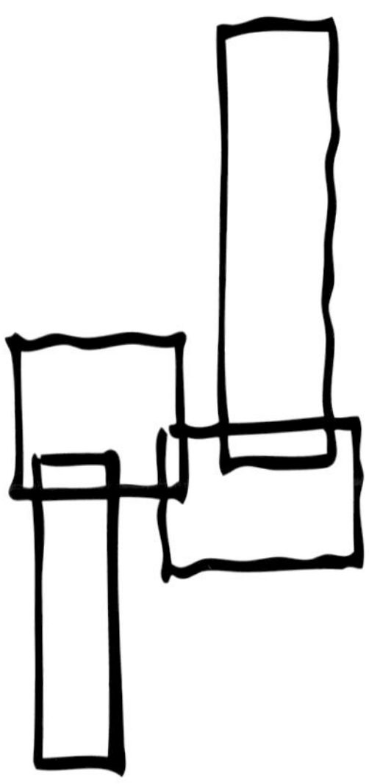

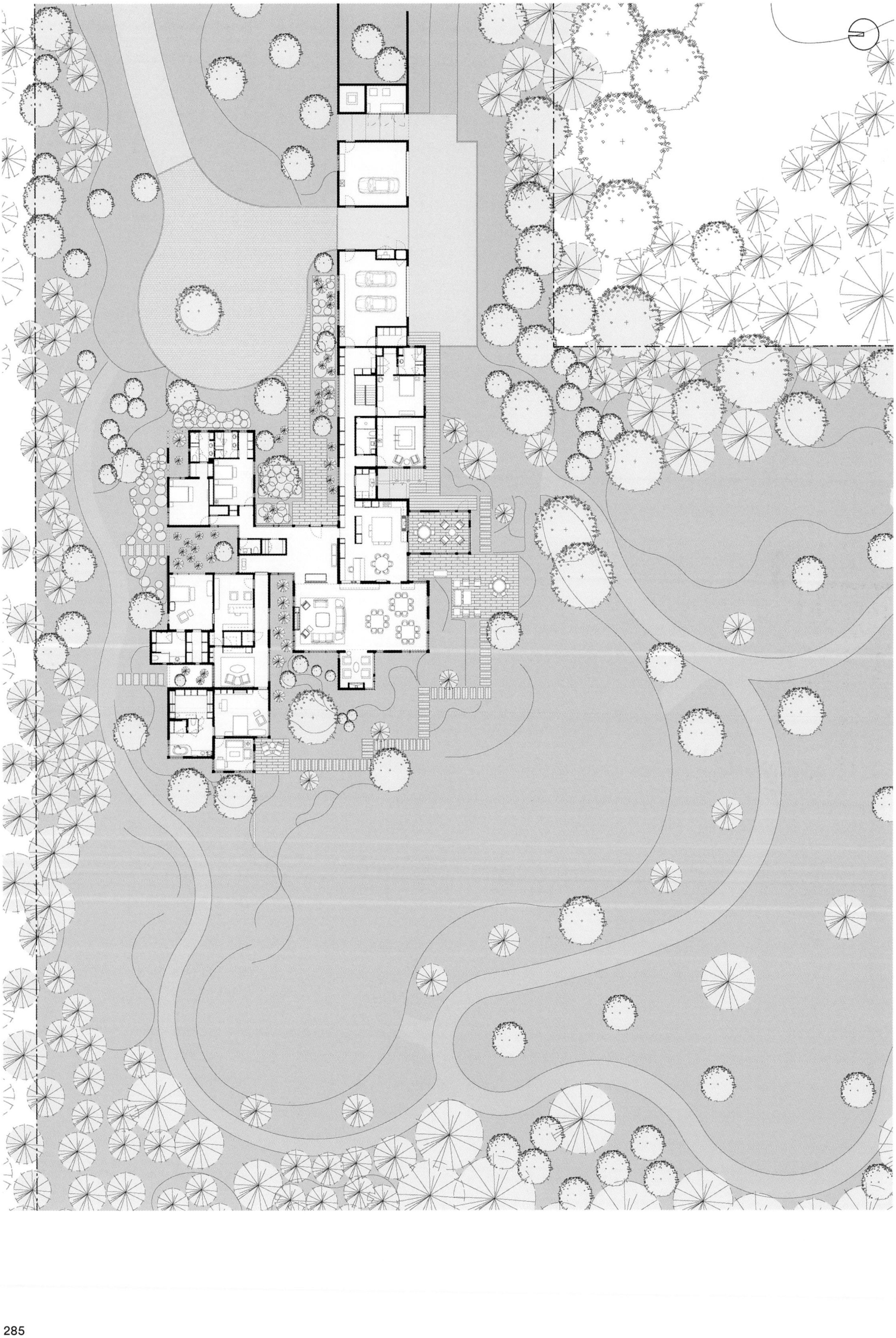

Midwest 2012

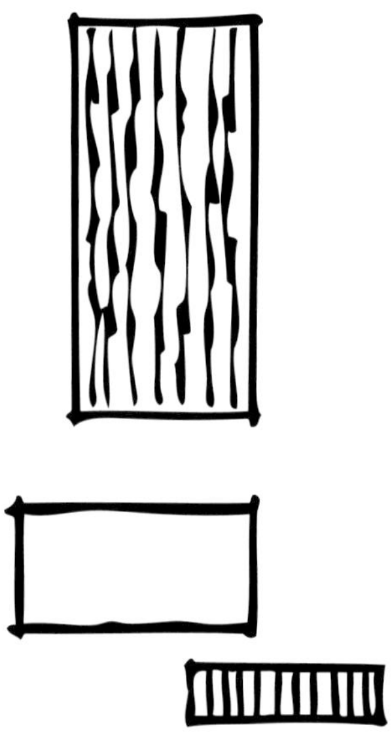

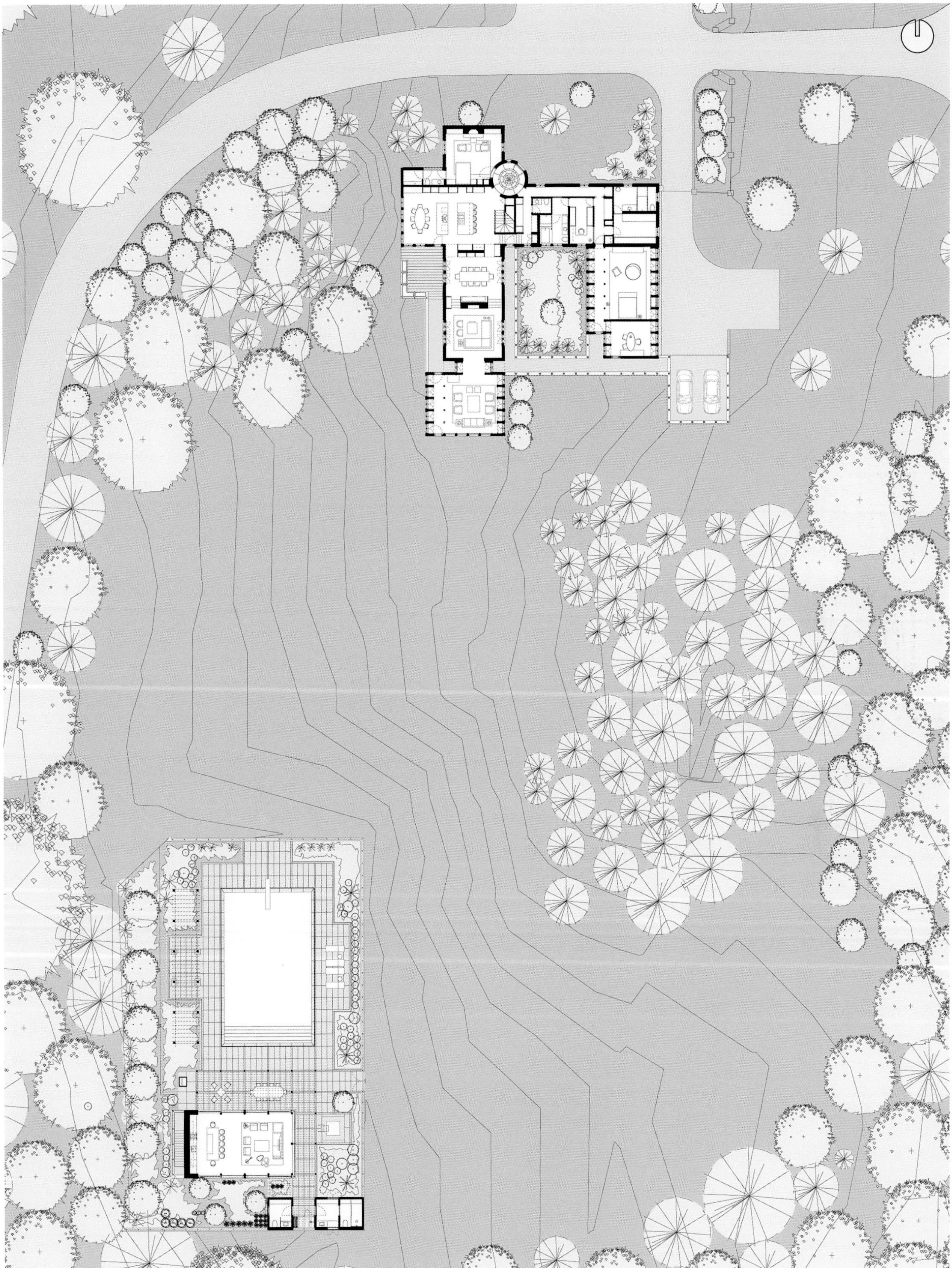

Oz Park 2011

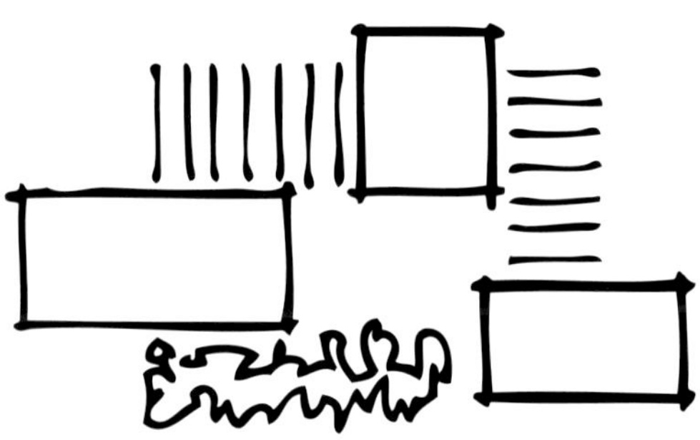

Marin 2004 / renovated 2015

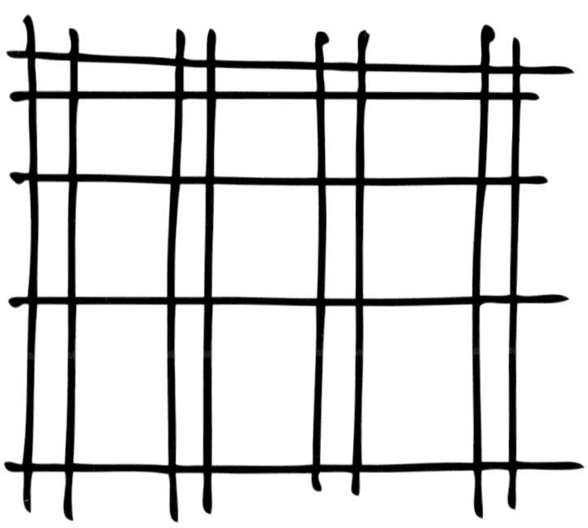

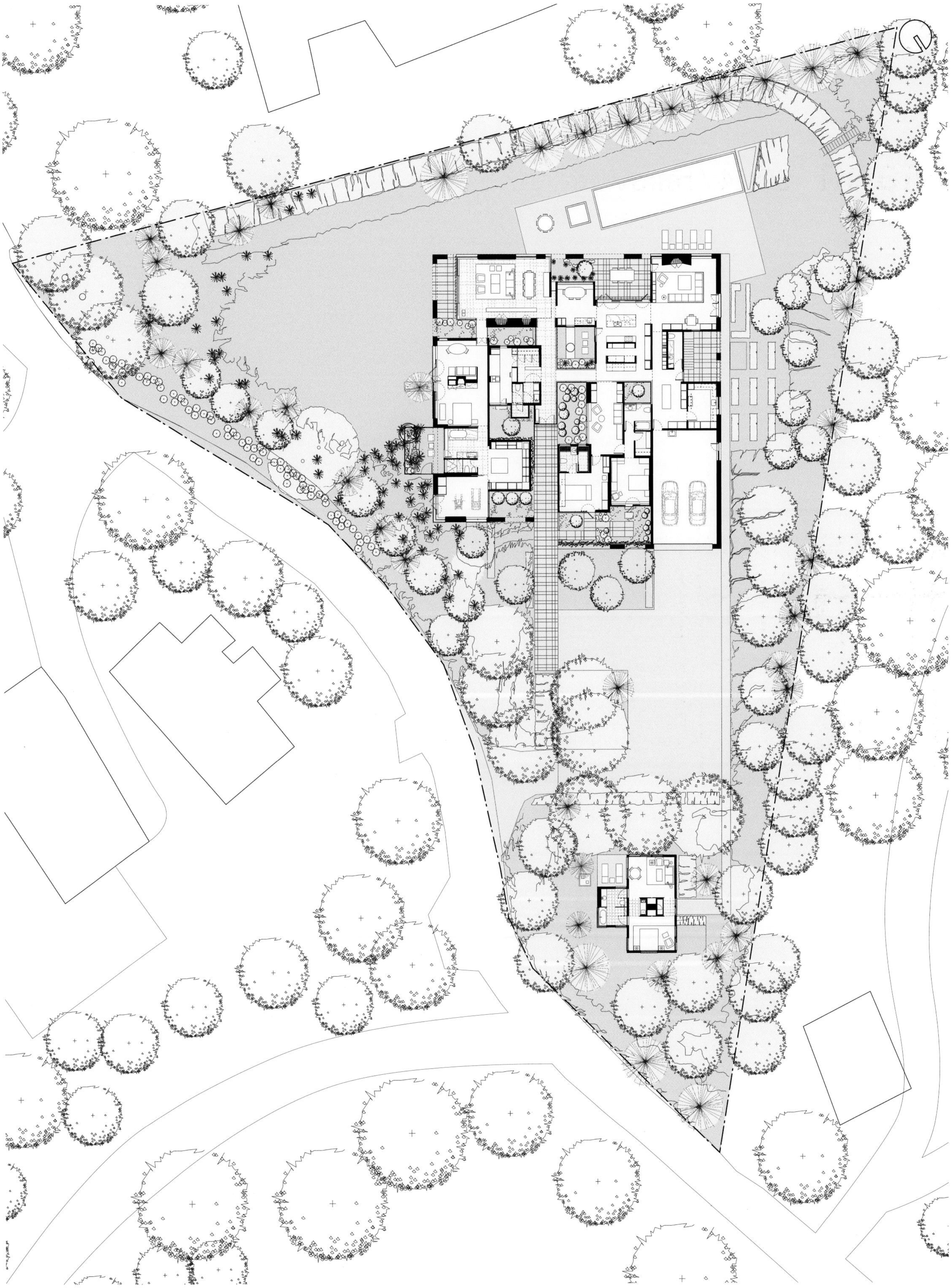

List of Illustrations and Image Credits

Dust jacket: Lake Michigan, Courtesy Dirk Denison Architects, Photo Hedrich Blessing Photographers | Tom Harris

Cover: Dirk Denison, Diagrammatic sketches for the houses published in this volume: (left to right, from top): Lake Michigan (2015), Carmel (2008), Wilmette (2010), Pine Lake (1991), Midwest (2012), Bucktown (2013), Bannockburn (2011), Westchester (2003), Marin (2004, renovated 2015), and Oz Park (2011), Courtesy Dirk Denison Architects

Frontispiece: Oz Park, Courtesy Dirk Denison Architects, Photo Michelle Litvin Studio

P. 10: Lake Michigan, Courtesy Dirk Denison Architects, Photo Bill Zbaren

P. 16: Marin, Courtesy Dirk Denison Architects, Photo Joshua McHugh

P. 18: Fig. 1, Foursquare house, Birmingham, Michigan, Courtesy Walter Denison

P. 19: Fig. 2, Frank Lloyd Wright, Melvyn Maxwell Smith and Sarah Stein Smith house (1950), Bloomfield Hills, Michigan, Courtesy Creative Commons, Photo Andrew Jameson / Fig. 3, Smith house, Interior, Courtesy James Haefner Photography, Inc.

P. 20: Fig. 4, Meathe, Kessler & Associates, Hilbert H. DeLawter house (1962), Bloomfield Hills, Michigan, Courtesy the Library of Congress, Photo Balthazar Korab

P. 21: Fig. 5, Meathe, Kessler & Associates, W. Hawkins Ferry house (1964), Grosse Point Shores, Michigan, Courtesy the Library of Congress, Photo Balthazar Korab / Fig. 6, Meathe, Kessler & Associates, W. Hawkins Ferry house, Interior, Courtesy University of Nebraska, Lincoln, Nebraska (UNL) Libraries

P. 22: Fig. 7, Frank O. Gehry, Easy Edges furniture line (1969–73), Courtesy Gehry Partners, LLP

P. 23: Fig. 8, Ellen Phelan, *Untitled (Blouse)* (ca. 1971), Paint on parchment, 30 × 19 1/4 in., Courtesy Ellen Phelan Studio, Photo Josh Nefsky / Fig. 9, Gordon Newton, *Untitled*, (1971), Edition 11/70, 40 × 52 in., Courtesy Dirk Denison Architects, Photo Devin Ehrenfried | Wright / Fig. 10, Aris Koutroulis, *1985 – #2A* (1985), Acrylic and canvas strips on canvas, 60 × 84 in., Courtesy Shannon's Fine Art Auctioneers, Photo Joseph Bartolomeo / Fig. 11, McArthur Binion, *dna: white painting: test for seasons XII* (2016), Oil paint stick and paper on board, 48 × 40 in., © McArthur Binion, Courtesy Galerie Lelong & Co.

P. 24: Fig. 12, Michael Heizer, *Dragged Mass Geometric* (1971), Detroit Institute of Arts, Detroit, Michigan, 18 March 1971, Courtesy Walter P. Reuther Library, Archives of Labor and Urban Affairs, Detroit News Collection, Wayne State University, Detroit, Michigan / Fig. 13, *Space Problem Dance*, IIT College of Architecture and Hubbard Street Dance Chicago Collaborative Studio (2008), Photo Tina Leto / Fig. 14, Mary Denison and Walter Denison at the opening of *Hair: The American Tribal Love-Rock Musical* (June 1970), Vest Pocket Theater, Detroit, Michigan, Courtesy Denison Family Archives

P. 25: Lake Michigan, Courtesy Dirk Denison Architects, Photo Bill Zbaren

Pp. 26-27 and 28-29: Lake Michigan, Courtesy Dirk Denison Architects, Photo Hedrich Blessing Photographers | Tom Harris

Pp. 30, 31, 32, 33, 34, 35 (top), 35 (bottom), 36-37, 38, 39, 40, 41, 42, 43 (left), 43 (right), 44–45, 47 and 48: Lake Michigan, Courtesy Dirk Denison Architects, Photo Eric Laignel

P. 46: Lake Michigan, Courtesy Dirk Denison Architects, Photo Tom Rossiter

P. 49: Fig. 15, Louis I. Kahn, Kimbell Art Museum, South Galleries (constructed 1969–72), Fort Worth, Texas, © 2013 Kimbell Art Museum, Fort Worth, Photo Robert LaPrelle / Fig. 16, Louis I. Kahn, Kimbell Art Museum, Courtyard, Courtesy OTTO, Photo Richard Barnes

P. 50: Fig. 17, Louis I. Kahn, Yale Center for British Art (completed 1977), Yale University, New Haven, Connecticut, Courtesy The Yale Center for British Art, Photo Richard Caspole / Fig. 18, Ludwig Mies van der Rohe, Farnsworth house (constructed 1945–51), Plano, Illinois, Courtesy the National Trust for Historic Preservation, Photo Akin Girav

P. 51: Fig. 19, Holabird & Root, Illinois Bell Telephone (IBT) Switching Station (1974), Northbrook, Illinois, Courtesy Holabird & Root, Photo Hedrich Blessing Photographers / Fig. 20, Skidmore, Owings & Merrill LLP, Willis Tower (1973), Chicago, Illinois, Courtesy SOM | Ezra Stoller © Esto, Photo Ezra Stoller / Fig. 21, Ludwig Mies van der Rohe, Federal Plaza, Chicago, Illinois, with Alexander Calder, *Flamingo* (1974), Courtesy Hagen Stier, Photo Hagen Stier

P. 52: Fig. 22, Ludwig Mies van der Rohe, S. R. Crown Hall (constructed 1950–56), Illinois Institute of Technology, Chicago, Illinois, HB-18506-Q4, Chicago History Museum, Hedrich-Blessing Collection © Chicago Historical Society, all rights reserved, Photo Hedrich Blessing Photographers / Fig. 23, Skidmore, Owings & Merrill LLP, The Republic Newspaper Office and Printing Plant, designed by Myron Goldsmith (1971), Columbus, Indiana, Courtesy the Library of Congress, Photo Balthazar Korab / Fig. 24, Ludwig Mies van der Rohe, Georg Schaefer Museum Project (1960–63), Schweinfurt, Germany, Interior perspective with view of site, Ink and photo collage with glass on illustration board, 30 × 40 in., © ARS, NY, Mies van der Rohe Archive, Gift of the architect, The Museum of Modern Art, New York, NY, Digital image © The Museum of Modern Art | Licensed by SCALA | Art Resource, NY

P. 53: Fig. 25, Skidmore, Owings & Merrill LLP, architect and structural engineer, McMath-Pierce Solar Telescope (1962), Kitt Peak National Observatory, Arizona, Courtesy SOM | Ezra Stoller © Esto, Photo Ezra Stoller / Fig. 26, Peter Eisenman, House X Model (1975), Courtesy Eisenman Architects

P. 54: Fig. 27, Denison cabin, Grayling, Michigan, Courtesy Walter Denison

P. 55: Fig. 28, Gilmore David Clark, Unisphere, 1964-65 New York *World's Fair*, Courtesy Creative Commons, Photo Anthony Conti / Fig. 29, Gilmore David Clark, Astral Fountain, 1964-65 New York *World's Fair,* Courtesy Walter Denison / Fig. 30, Victor Lundy, *Space Flowers* on roof of Brass Rail lunch bar with observation platform towers, New York State Pavilion, 1964-65 New York *World's Fair,* © Associated Press, Courtesy AP Images, Photo Marty Lederhandler

P. 56: Fig. 31, R. Buckminster Fuller, Biosphère, U.S. Pavilion, *EXPO '67*, Montréal, Québec, Canada, Courtesy Science Photo Library, Photo Jimmy Fox / Fig. 32, Moshe Safdie, Habitat 67, *EXPO '67*, Montréal, Québec, Canada, Courtesy Consulat, Photo Alexi Hobbs

Pp. 57, 58, 59, 61, 62-63, 64-65, 67, 68, 69, 70 and 71: Carmel, Courtesy Dirk Denison Architects, Photo David Matheson Photography

P. 72: Carmel, Courtesy Kathy Bang, Photo Kathy Bang

P. 73: Fig. 33, Ponte Vecchio, Florence, Italy, Courtesy Shutterstock, Photo Danilo Ascione / Fig. 34, Pantheon, Rome, Italy, Photo Public Domain

P. 74: Fig. 35, Dirk Denison on the porch of a cabin, Grand Canyon National Park, Arizona, Courtesy Walter Denison / Fig. 36, Hôtel de N'Gor, Dakar, Senegal, Postcard, Courtesy Denison Family Archives

P. 75: Fig. 37, Victoria Falls, Zambezi River, Zambia–Zimbabwe border, Courtesy Shutterstock, Photo Paul Murtagh

P. 76: Fig. 38, Frei Otto and Günther Behnisch, Olympiastadion (1968–72), Munich, Germany, Courtesy Flickr, Photo Chris & Lori / Fig. 39, Joseph Nathaniel French of Albert Kahn Associates, Fisher Building (1928), Detroit, Michigan, Courtesy Manning Brothers Historic Photographic Collection

P. 77: Fig. 40, Joseph Nathaniel French of Albert Kahn Associates, Fisher Building, Interior (1928), Detroit, Michigan, Courtesy James Haefner Photography, Inc., Photo James Haefner Photography, Inc. / Fig. 41, Rivera Court, Detroit Institute of Arts, Detroit, Michigan, with Diego Rivera fresco cycle depicting Detroit Industry (1932–33), Courtesy Detroit Institute of Arts, Gift of Edsel B. Ford, Bridgeman Images

P. 78: Fig. 42, Albert Kahn, General Motors Headquarters, Durant and Cadillac Place Buildings (1922), Detroit, Michigan, Courtesy Albert Kahn Associates, Inc. / Fig. 43, Albert Kahn, Detroit Athletic Club (1915), Detroit, Michigan, © Jason Robinson Photography

P. 79: Fig. 44, Minoru Yamasaki with Smith, Hinchman & Grylls, Michigan Consolidated Gas Company Building (now One Woodward Avenue, completed 1963), Detroit, Michigan, Photo David Holowka, ArchiTakes.com / Fig. 45, Michigan Consolidated Gas Company Building, Courtesy the Library of Congress, Photo Balthazar Korab / Fig. 46, Smith, Hinchman & Grylls, First Federal Savings and Loan Association Building (1965), © Detroit Free Press, ZUMA, Photo Bert Emanuele

Pp. 81, 82-83, 84-85, 86, 87, 88-89, 90 (left), 90 (right), 91, 92-93, 94, 95 and 96: Wilmette, Courtesy Dirk Denison Architects, Photo Michelle Litvin Studio

P. 97: Fig. 47, Eero Saarinen, TWA Flight Center (1962), JFK International Airport, New York, NY, Courtesy the Library of Congress, Photo Balthazar Korab / Fig. 48, Kevin Roche John Dinkeloo and Associates, LLC (Roche Dinkeloo), Ford Foundation Headquarters (1968), New York, NY, © David Leventi | Courtesy Rick Wester Fine Art, Photo David Leventi

P. 98: Fig. 49, Skidmore, Owings & Merrill, Beinecke Library (1963), Yale University, New Haven, Connecticut, © Ezra Stoller | Esto, Photo Ezra Stoller / Fig. 50, Minoru Yamasaki, McGregor Memorial Conference Center (1958), Wayne State University, Detroit, Michigan, Courtesy Archives of Michigan, Photo D. Bartush

P. 99: Fig. 51, Minoru Yamasaki with Smith, Hinchman & Grylls, Michigan Consolidated Gas Company Building (now One Woodward Avenue, completed 1963), Detroit, Michigan, Courtesy Creative Commons, Photo Michael S. Russell / Fig. 52, Minoru Yamasaki and his assistant in his studio reviewing model for World Trade Center, Courtesy The Library of Congress, Photo Balthazar Korab

P. 100: Fig. 53, Map of the Cranbrook campus, Bloomfield Hills, Michigan, © Cranbrook Educational Community

P. 101: Fig. 54, Eliel Saarinen, Cranbrook Academy of Art, Triton Pools (1916), with Carl Milles sculptures, Courtesy Cranbrook Archives, BKA1, Photo Balthazar Korab (ca. 1985) / Fig. 55, Carl Milles, Cranbrook Academy of Art, Orpheus Fountain, © Cranbrook Archives, AA2354-1, Photo Harvey Croze (September 1948) / Fig. 56, Eliel Saarinen, Cranbrook Academy of Art, Library (1942), Courtesy the Library of Congress, Photo Balthazar Korab

P. 102: Fig. 57, Eliel Saarinen, Cranbrook School for Boys (1928), Courtesy the Library of Congress, Photo Balthazar Korab / Fig. 58, Eliel Saarinen, Kingswood School for Girls (1931), Green Lobby Stair, © Cranbrook Center for Collections and Research | James Haefner, Photo James Haefner Photography, Inc. / Fig. 59, Eliel Saarinen, Kingswood School for Girls (1931), Courtesy Brian Callahan | Flickr, Photo Brian Callahan

P. 103: Fig. 60, Eliel Saarinen, Cranbrook School, Dining Hall (1928), © Cranbrook Archives, N53, Photo Peter A. Nyholm

Pp. 105, 106-107, 108, 109, 110-111, 112, 113, 115 and 116: Pine Lake, Courtesy Dirk Denison Architects, Photo Balthazar Korab

P. 117: Fig. 61, John Dinkeloo, Roche Dinkeloo, Power Center for the Performing Arts (1971), University of Michigan, Ann Arbor, Michigan, Courtesy Kevin Roche John Dinkeloo and Associates LLC / Fig. 62, Gunnar Birkerts and Associates, The Allan and Alene Smith Law Library Addition (1981), University of Michigan, Ann Arbor, Michigan, Photo Janet Pickel

P. 118: Fig. 63, *Geometric Series in Base 3*, Ink on Strathmore, Courtesy Dirk Denison Architects / Fig. 64, *Visual and Mathematical Matrix*, Ink on Strathmore, Courtesy Dirk Denison Architects

P. 119, Fig. 65, *Mass and Voids*, Collage on Strathmore, Courtesy Dirk Denison Architects / Fig. 66, *Planes in Space*, Collage on Strathmore, Courtesy Dirk Denison Architects / Fig. 67, *Warped Planes*, Ink on Strathmore, Courtesy Dirk Denison Architects / Fig. 68, *Color, Texture, and Their Relationship*, Collage on Strathmore, Courtesy Dirk Denison Architects

P. 120: Fig. 69, *Housing Studies*, Plans, Graphite on Strathmore, Courtesy Dirk Denison Architects / Fig. 70, *The Space Problem*, Interior perspective, Collage on Strathmore, Courtesy Dirk Denison Architects

P. 121: Fig. 71, *The Space Problem*, Model (exterior), Scale: ¼ in. = 1 ft. 0 in., Courtesy Dirk Denison Architects, Photo Balthazar Korab / Fig. 72, *The Space Problem*, Model (interior), Scale: ¼ in. = 1 ft. 0 in., Courtesy Dirk Denison Architects, Photo Balthazar Korab

P. 122: Fig. 73, *Annex to the College of Architecture, Planning and Design, IIT*, Model, (exterior), Courtesy Dirk Denison Architects, Photo Balthazar Korab / Fig. 74, *Annex to the College of Architecture, Planning and Design, IIT*, Model (interior), Courtesy Dirk Denison Architects, Photo Balthazar Korab

P. 123: Fig. 75, Ludwig Mies van der Rohe, Library and Administration Building Proposal, Illinois Institute of Technology, Chicago, Illinois (ca. 1944), Charcoal, graphite, and yellow pencil on tracing paper, 28¾ × 42 in., © ARS, NY, Restricted Gift of the Auxiliary Board of The Art Institute of Chicago, Chicago, Illinois, 1987.46, Courtesy The Art Institute of Chicago, Art Resource, NY / Fig. 76, Ludwig Mies van der Rohe Library and Administration Building, Perspective drawing for southeast corner (ca. 1944–45), Pencil on tracing paper, 44 × 34 in., Delineator, Sing Mau Chau, Mies van der Rohe Archive, Gift of the architect, The Museum of Modern Art, New York, NY, Digital image © The Museum of Modern Art, Licensed by SCALA, Art Resource, NY

Pp. 124-125: Fig. 77, *Geometric Studies*, Graphite on Strathmore, Courtesy Dirk Denison Architects

P. 126: Fig. 78, *20th & Market*, M. Arch Thesis project for an 80-story tower, Plans, Graphite on Strathmore, Courtesy Dirk Denison Architects

P. 127: Fig. 79, *20th & Market*, M. Arch Thesis project for an 80-story tower, Elevations and sections, Graphite on Strathmore, Courtesy Dirk Denison Architects

P. 128: Fig. 80, Le Corbusier, Carpenter Center for the Visual Arts (1963), Harvard University, Cambridge, Massachusetts, Courtesy the Carpenter Center for the Visual Arts, Harvard University

Pp. 129, 130-131, 132-133, 135, 136, 137, 138-139, 140, 141, 142-143 and 144: Westchester, Courtesy Dirk Denison Architects, Photo Joshua McHugh

P. 146: Fig. 81, Pine Lake, Courtesy Dirk Denison Architects, Photo Dirk Denison

P. 147: Fig. 82, Pine Lake, Plan, Ink on mylar, Courtesy Dirk Denison Architects

P. 148: Fig. 83, Lake Michigan, Courtesy Dirk Denison Architects, Photo Roaming Badger

P. 149: Fig. 84, Lake Michigan, Courtesy Dirk Denison Architects, Photo Tom Rossiter

P. 150: Figs. 85 and 86, Bannockburn, Courtesy Dirk Denison Architects, Photo Michelle Litvin Studio

P. 152: Fig. 87, Carmel, Courtesy Dirk Denison Architects, Photo David Matheson Photography

Pp. 153, 154-155, 156-157, 158, 159, 161, 162-163, 165, 166, 167 and 168: Bucktown, Courtesy Dirk Denison Architects, Photo Tom Rossiter

P. 164: Bucktown, Courtesy Dirk Denison Architects, Photo Dirk Denison Architects

P. 169: Fig. 88, Marin, Courtesy Dirk Denison Architects, Photo David Matheson Photography

P. 170: Fig. 89, Marin, Courtesy Dirk Denison Architects, Photo Joshua McHugh

P. 171: Figs. 90 and 91, Wilmette, Courtesy Dirk Denison Architects, Photo Michelle Litvin Studio

Pp. 172 and 173: Figs. 92, 93 and 94, Westchester, Courtesy Dirk Denison Architects, Photo Joshua McHugh

P. 174: Fig. 95, Bucktown, Courtesy Dirk Denison Architects, Photo Tom Rossiter

P. 175: Fig. 96, Midwest, Courtesy Dirk Denison Architects, Photo George Lambros, Lambros Photography, Inc.

P. 176: Figs. 97 and 98, Oz Park, Courtesy Dirk Denison Architects, Photo Michelle Litvin Studio

Pp. 177, 178-179, 180-181, 182, 183, 184-185, 186-187 and 188: Bannockburn, Courtesy Dirk Denison Architects, Photo Michelle Litvin Studio

P. 189: Fig. 99, Pine Lake, Collage, Ink and photo on paper, Courtesy Dirk Denison Architects

P. 190: Fig. 100, Westchester, Courtesy Dirk Denison Architects, Photo Joshua McHugh

P. 191: Fig. 101, Lake Michigan, Courtesy Dirk Denison Architects, Photo Hedrich Blessing Photographers | Tom Harris

P. 192: Fig. 102, Lake Michigan, Courtesy Dirk Denison Architects, Photo Bill Zbaren

P. 193: Fig. 103, Pine Lake, Courtesy Dirk Denison Architects, Photo Balthazar Korab

P. 194: Fig. 104, Lake Michigan, Courtesy Dirk Denison Architects, Photo Bill Zbaren

Pp. 194-195: Fig. 105, Marin, *Measured Rhythm*, Graphite on Strathmore, Courtesy Dirk Denison Architects

P. 196: Fig. 106, Marin, Courtesy Dirk Denison Architects, Photo Joshua McHugh

Pp. 197, 198-199, 200-201, 202, 203, 207 and 208: Midwest, Courtesy Dirk Denison Architects, Photo George Lambros, Lambros Photography, Inc.

Pp. 204, 205 and 206: Midwest, Courtesy Dirk Denison Architects, Photo Michelle Litvin Studio

P. 209: Fig. 107, Oz Park, Courtesy Dirk Denison Architects, Photo Michelle Litvin Studio

P. 211: Figs. 108, 109, 110 and 111, Bannockburn, Models for variant schemes, Museum board, Courtesy Dirk Denison Architects, Photo Dirk Denison Architects

P. 212: Fig. 112, Pine Lake, Courtesy Dirk Denison Architects, Photo Balthazar Korab

P. 213: Fig. 113, Bannockburn, Courtesy Dirk Denison Architects, Photo Michelle Litvin Studio

P. 214: Fig. 114, Wilmette, Courtesy Dirk Denison Architects, Photo Michelle Litvin Studio

P. 215: Fig. 115, Denison & Salkin Apartment, Terrarium, Photo David Salkin

P. 216: Fig. 116, Oz Park, Courtesy Dirk Denison Architects, Photo Michelle Litvin Studio

Pp. 217, 218-219, 220, 221, 222-223, 224, 225, 226, 227, 228-229, 230, 231, 232-233, 235, 236-237, 239 and 240: Oz Park, Courtesy Dirk Denison Architects, Photo Michelle Litvin Studio

P. 241: Fig. 117, Marin, Courtesy Dirk Denison Architects, Photo David Matheson Photography

P. 242: Fig. 118, Chicago Apartment, Custom coffee table (2010), Marble, bronze, and glass, Courtesy Dirk Denison Architects, Photo Michelle Litvin Studio / Fig. 119, Lake Michigan, Custom coffee table (2013), Stone, acrylic, and lacquered wood, Courtesy Dirk Denison Architects, Photo Dirk Denison Architects

P. 243: Fig. 120, Lake Michigan, Custom dining table (2013), Aluminum and translucent acrylic, Courtesy Dirk Denison Architects, Photo Tom Rossiter / Fig. 121, Wilmette, Custom dining table (2009), Aluminum and Durat, Courtesy Dirk Denison Architects, Photo Michelle Litvin Studio / Fig. 122, Washington, D.C. Apartment, Custom dining table (2016), Stainless steel and translucent acrylic, Courtesy Dirk Denison Architects, Photo Eric Laignel

P. 244: Fig. 123, Chicago Apartment, Custom dining table (2010), Courtesy Dirk Denison Architects, Photo Michelle Litvin Studio / Fig. 124, Oz Park, Custom dining table (2011), Wood and translucent acrylic, Courtesy Dirk Denison Architects, Photo Michelle Litvin Studio / Fig. 125, Oz Park, Custom dining table (2011), Detail, Wood, Courtesy Dirk Denison Architects, Photo Michelle Litvin Studio

P. 245: Fig. 126, Washington, D.C. Apartment, Wolfgang Tillmans, *Urgency XXIX* (2006), Chromogenic print mounted on Dibond aluminum in artist's frame, Edition 1 of 1, 93¾ × 71¼ × 2¼ in., Courtesy Dirk Denison Architects, Photo Eric Laignel

P. 246: Fig. 127, Chicago Apartment, Jim Hodges, *here it comes* (2009), Charcoal, 24K gold, pastel, saliva on paper in 7 parts, 30¼ × 179 in. overall, Courtesy Dirk Denison Architects, Photo Michelle Litvin Studio / Fig. 128, Pine Lake, Michele Oka Doner, *Doppler* (1991), Cast bronze installation, Courtesy Michele Oka Doner / Fig. 129, Lake Michigan, Michele Oka Doner, *Telchine* (2013), Cast bronze fountain, 77 × 23 × 27 in., Courtesy Michele Oka Doner, Photo Hedrich Blessing Photographers

P. 247: Fig. 130, Chicago Office, Máximo González, *Dream* (2006), Collage, Out-of-circulation international currency cut up and mounted directly on the wall, Courtesy Máximo González, Photo Máximo González / Fig. 131, Bucktown, Beverly Fishman, *Untitled* (2015), Urethane paint on wood, 60 × 60 × 2¼ in., Courtesy Dirk Denison Architects, Photo Tom Rossiter

P. 248: Fig. 132, Marin, Harry Bertoia, *Untitled (Somnambient)* (ca. 1965), Courtesy Dirk Denison Architects, Photo David Matheson Photography

Pp. 249, 253, 263 and 268: Marin, Courtesy Dirk Denison Architects, Photo Joshua McHugh

Pp. 250-251, 252, 254-255, 256-257, 258, 259, 261, 262, 264, 265 and 266-267: Marin, Courtesy Dirk Denison Architects, Photo David Matheson Photography

P. 273: Lake Michigan, Site plan drawing, Courtesy Dirk Denison Architects

P. 275: Carmel, Site plan drawing, Courtesy Dirk Denison Architects

P. 277: Wilmette, Site plan drawing, Courtesy Dirk Denison Architects

P. 279: Pine Lake, Site plan drawing, Courtesy Dirk Denison Architects

P. 281: Westchester, Site plan drawing, Courtesy Dirk Denison Architects

P. 283: Bucktown, Site plan drawing, Courtesy Dirk Denison Architects

P. 285: Bannockburn, Site plan drawing, Courtesy Dirk Denison Architects

P. 287, Midwest, Site plan drawing, Courtesy Dirk Denison Architects

P. 289, Oz Park, Site plan drawing, Courtesy Dirk Denison Architects

P. 291, Marin, Site plan drawing, Courtesy Dirk Denison Architects

Dirk Denison **10 Houses**

Publisher
Actar
New York / Barcelona
www.actar.com

Editor
Denise Bratton

Project Manager
Tyler Waldorf, Dirk Denison Architects

Consultant
David Salkin Creative

Graphic Design
Lorraine Wild and Xiaoqing Wang
of Green Dragon Office, Los Angeles

Production
Professional Graphics Inc., Rockford, Illinois
Tiger Printing Company, Ltd, China

This book was typeset by Green Dragon Office in Circular Pro, designed by Laurenz Brunner, and Memphis, designed by Rudolf Wolf.

Distribution
Actar D, Inc.

New York
440 Park Avenue South, 17th Floor
New York, NY 10016, USA
+1 212 966 2207
salesnewyork@actar-d.com

Barcelona
Roca i Batlle 2-4
08023 Barcelona, Spain
+34 933 282 183
eurosales@actar-d.com

English ISBN: 978-1-945150-75-3
PCN: Library of Congress Control Number
2017956613

A CIP catalogue record for this book is available from the Library of Congress, Washington, D.C., USA.

Printed in China, July 2018